The ART and CRAFT of RIBBON WORK

edited by Jules & Kaethe Kliot

LACIS PUBLICATIONS

Berkeley, California

SOURCE FOR SUPPLIES

LACIS,   2982 Adeline Street,   Berkeley, CA 94703
Ribbons, books, floral, millinery and costume supplies,
"Quick Crafter" ribbon   tools, floral irons. ..
Send $4.00 for complete catalog.

LACIS

PUBLICATIONS

3163 Adeline Street, Berkeley, CA 94703

© 1993, Jules Kliot
ISBN 0-916896-51-X

The Romance of Silk Ribbons

HUNDREDS of years ago, Ribbon, favorite daughter of Silk, Queen of Textiles, was born. Born, truly, for you know, the original "ribband" of our remote forefathers was not a distinct, narrow silken web. It was but a stripe in a material, or the band or border of a garment, whether woven in the piece or not.

The imaginative enterprise of the aesthethic Frenchman conceived Silk Ribbon as a distinct form. In the eleventh century, the weaving of the sheeny strand was begun near St. Etienne in the Department of the Loire, France.

For a few hundred years afterward the manufacture of Silk Ribbon languished. Then, in the 16th century, came the invention of the self-acting Ribbon Loom which permitted the weaving of several webs at one time.

Since that time, the history of ribbon has been honorable and useful and romantic.

It has graced the slender throats and embellished the dainty insteps of all the lovely women of France—of Maintenon, Pompadour and Marie Antoinette.

Shakespeare sang of Ribbon: "Get your apparel together, good strings to your beards, new ribbons to your pumps."

Ribbon became a patent of nobility, the badge of distinction of orders of knighthood. The Knights of the Garter selected the blue and the Knights of the Bath the red.

It even gave its name to Ribbonism, the famous secret society movement in Ireland whose supporters were distinguished by the wearing of a green ribbon badge.

Ribbon supplanted the laurel of the ancients as the supreme reward for victory.

But throughout all the years, Ribbon's chief glory has been the adornment of lovely womankind.

In the performance of this service it stands today as the fabric form most elastic and most various in its uses, most distinctive ornamentally and most significant in its symbolism.

from RIBBONOLOGY

from RIBBONOLOGY

INTRODUCTION

The ribbon has long fascinated designers and craftsmen as one of the more important materials of ornament. Used as a bold ornament for the hair as well as the subtle hidden ornament for lingerie, the ribbon can be purely decorative or serve as the necessary tie to keep a garment or accessory in place. it is difficult to find any period of costume where ribbon is not a element of design.

In addition to the free forming of the basic ribbon into floral and bow forms, ribbon was also uses as the basic material for creation of realistic flowers. Here the ribbon was cut into specific shapes, embossed with a hot iron and combined with stamens and calyx to form these displays. Ribbon also found its was as a new media for the embroiderer, In addition to simply using it in lieu of thread, it could be gathered, twisted and manipulated in other ways to create a new form of dimensional embroidery.

With the perfection of ribbon manufacturing techniques during the early part of this century, and the simple lines of dress appearing in the 20's , the ribbon took on an important role as the prime costume accessory. The ribbon techniques which evolved from the great Edwardian millinery styles were now refined and perfected for this new era.

One of the more important guides, published during this period was **THE ART AND CRAFT OF RIBBON WORK**, originally published in 1918 by The Illustrated Milliner Co. This first edition of this book is reproduced in this volume in its entirety with the exception of the color plates (pgs 16, 18, 19 and 20) which are here reproduced in black and white.

Additional materials are included from the very popular **RIBBON ART**, Vol. I, No. III published by the Ribbon Art Publishing Company (no date) and. **RIBBONOLOGY**, a romantic perspective of ribbon published by Johnson-Cowdid-Emmerich, Inc. (no date), an annual illustrating the practical use of ribbons

Today, a tremendous revival of ribbon work in both the techniques of folding and embroidery is taking place. The variety of ribbons in terms of style, color and widths is as extensive as it has ever been and the new interest in millinery has further expanded interest in ribbon techniques.

Jules & Kaethe Kliot

CONTENTS

THE ART AND CRAFT OF RIBBON WORK   7
     Index   65
RIBBON ART   66
     Directions for Making Trimmings   66
     Five Ways of Trimming the Same Hat   67
     Easy to Follow Instructions   68
RIBBONOLOGY   82
     The Seven Ages of Ribbons   83

BIBLIOGRAPHY

Additional sources for the study of ribbon manipulation are offered below. Most can be obtained from this publisher:

EASY RIBBONCRAFT, Juanne Strayss

FASHIONS IN TRIM: WISH BOOK XXIV, Susan Sirkis

HATS ON HEADS, Mildred Anlezark

MILLINERY FOR EVERY WOMAN, Georgina Kerr Kaye

OLD FASHIONED RIBBON ART, Ribbon Art Co.

OLD FASHIONES RIBBON TRIMMINGS & FLOWERS, Mary Brooks Picken

RIBBON ART TECHNIQUES (Japanese text), Emiko Takahashi

RIBBON TRIMMINGS, A COURSE IN SIX PARTS, Woman's Institute of Domestic Arts & Sciences, Dept. of Millinery

GUIDES FOR THE RIBBON CRAFTER TOOL:, Pam Stiegeler

BOWS MADE EASY, FASHION BOWS FOR THE HAIR, MAKING RIBBON FLOWERS 1, MAKING RIBBON FLOWERS 2

A Flower from the Garden of Dress

FOUNDATION OF GOWN MADE OF PINK CHIFFON, WITH THREE PASTEL COLORINGS OF LADY FAIR RIBBON JOINED TOGETHER WITH ONE-INCH HAND-MADE LACE, PUFFINGS OF A PALE PINK RIBBON, 615 QUALITY. CORSAGE IS MADE OF SEVEN DIFFERENT SHADINGS OF LADY FAIR RIBBON FORMED INTO BLOSSOMS. HAT IS MADE OF PALE PINK MOHAIR BRAID, TRIMMED WITH SIMILAR BLOSSOMS AS ON CORSAGE; STREAMERS OF WIDE MAIS AND PINK LADY FAIR RIBBON. PARASOL OF PALE PINK TAFFETA, TRIMMED WITH SIMILAR BLOSSOMS AS ON CORSAGE.

from RIBBONOLOGY

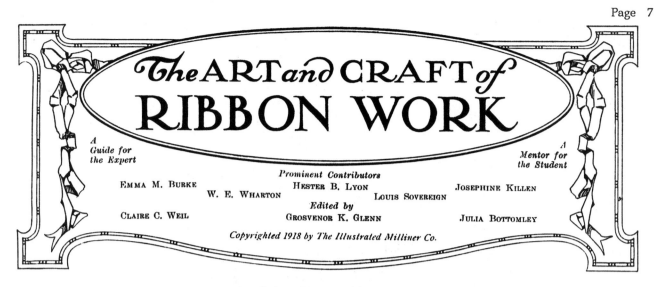

The ART and CRAFT of RIBBON WORK

A Guide for the Expert

A Mentor for the Student

Prominent Contributors

Emma M. Burke   Hester B. Lyon   Josephine Killen

W. E. Wharton   Louis Sovereign

Edited by

Claire C. Weil   Grosvenor K. Glenn   Julia Bottomley

Copyrighted 1918 by The Illustrated Milliner Co.

INTRODUCTORY

There is an art in the handling of ribbon which is well recognized. In popular vernacular it is spoken of as the "knack." This art on the part of the bowmaker finds its highest expression in the ability to complete the article with the freshness and elegance of the ribbon retained, and showing no trace of its having been handled. In other words, a master of the craft creates ribbon ornaments of varied character without impairing the beauty and lustre of the fabric.

Those who, blessed by nature, possess the art of manipulating ribbons, will find a new delight in their art by adopting the short processes taught in this volume, for producing difficult designs. Many intricate bows and ornaments, by old methods only possible to produce by masters of the craft, have been simplified by the science of these same ingenious master craftsmen and made comparatively easy to construct.

The person not endowed with that rare ability, craftsmanship in ribbon work, may quickly acquire a wonderful efficiency by following the steps given in the instructive descriptions for developing ribbon ornaments given herein. In no other art is it more true than in the Craft of Ribbon Work that "Practice Makes Perfect."

The craft of ribbon work embraces many branches, for the field of usefulness of ribbons has been widened until they have become indispensable in all lines of women's and children's apparel. The bowmaker progresses and develops into an expert manipulator of ribbon, an artist of the craft. The products of the artists have become an important factor in house equipment and interior decoration.

The use of ribbon marks an increasing advance in standards of living and dressing and these standards grow more and more artistic year by year.

The Art and Craft of Ribbon Work embraces the various uses of ribbon in the domestic and decorative arts. It is the most exhaustive and comprehensive volume devoted to the manipulation of ribbon yet compiled. The illustrations of a multitude of attractive and effective developments from ribbons will stimulate the creative ability of the expert and with the detailed instructions for making them will be the mentor of the student.

The Art and Craft of Ribbon Work will be found practically indispensable to any ribbon department and will prove invaluable to any merchant or milliner selling ribbons.

Ribbons in Millinery

Ribbons form an essential part of every stock of millinery goods, and it is necessary for every milliner to have some ability in manipulating ribbons.

Hand and Machine Made Bows

The Art and Craft of Ribbon Work places particular emphasis upon the many ways in which ribbon may be used in millinery. The different types of millinery bows and ornaments are accurately illustrated and fully described. These millinery decorations have been carefully assorted and grouped in their separate classes for convenient reference and easy comparison. They include hand-made bows and ornaments for dress and semi-dress hats, and machine-made trimming motifs suitable for tailored, sport, trimmed and dress hats. The machine-made ornaments enable a single operator to produce enormous quantities of these garnitures per day. The detailed descriptions will enable the least experienced needle-woman at home, in the millinery workroom or factory to reproduce the patterns that suit one's individual fancy.

Ribbon Flowers

The same thing is true of the ribbon flowers. Each successive step in their construction is shown by photographs. The ribbon maker having mastered the details of a single rose by any of the methods shown, can use her acquired knowledge in fashioning any kind of rose, taking her models from nature.

Prepared for Experts

The contents of this volume represents a most careful and judicious selection of the choicest designs produced by the acknowledged masters in the craft of ribbon work. It has been compiled for the benefit of experts who are actively engaged in handling ribbons daily. Of necessity it is absolutely accurate and may be relied upon as a book of instruction *par excellence* for the novice in the workroom and the student in the classroom. It was edited with the definite object of making it a reference book establishing standards of practice in the trades using ribbons.

Lessons in Rose Making
Detailing the Development from Stem to full-blown Flower

These various roses are all of original design and were evolved by Mrs. E. M. Burke, San Francisco, Cal., for her Millinery Classes from studies of the dainty flowers themselves. Pistils for flower centers, calyxes and seed pods of various kinds for the base of the flowers, next the stems, and leaves, buds and stems, may be obtained from supply houses in almost every city.

California is essentially the home of the perfect rose. The finest varieties, that grow only in hothouses in the East, here flourish in the open air. Over thirty-three years' study and cultivation of them has led to these reproductions in ribbon. Some of their features are conventionalized; some are not exactly true to nature, but these variations arise from the necessity of developing greater beauty in the ribbon. The natural rose needs no addition to its loveliness.

For instance, the full blown rose has no pistils or stamens, they having been changed into its multitudinous petals. We find the ribbon rose has an added grace by placing a few stamens, almost hidden, in its center, despite the fact that this means a departure from nature.

On the other hand, the Cherokee rose is made as near like the true one as it is possible for artifice to do it.

The Large Full-Blown Rose—(See B, Page 13)

Use No. 5 Millinery needles and 24D millinery thread for sewing on the petals, but the pink thread for the construction of the petals and the green thread used on the calyx are both No. 50—not the mercerized, but hard twisted, and never use silk, it will slip. The needles for this thread are No. 8 sharps.

This rose takes 2⅔ yards of No. 12 ribbon. It is beautiful in yellow, pink or dark red. Cut off 8 petals, length 4 inches; 8 petals, length 4½ inches; 5 petals, length 5 inches.

Double the petal ribbon, turn down the corners as at "1," roll it over again as at "2"; insert the left thumb lightly between the folds of the ribbon, and hold the roll between the thumb and the left forefinger—do not crush or crease the roll. Open up the ribbon and stitch from the inside as shown in "3." You can see through the ribbon so as to insert the needle, and catch the roll in its hollow near the edge, but be careful that the stitches do not come through on the right side. Catch in the second place and turn the ribbon on the right side again, and make the second roll, which hold and secure as the first. Never break the thread in making the two rolls. The upper part of all petals is made in the same way and after a little practice can be done easily.

Make a crease by overlapping at the bottom as in "4," and secure it by running a straight thread across its lower edge. Fold all the petals in the same direction and with only one fold. The place where the petal cups out most should be in the middle of it, for the center of the rose, which is made

of the first 8 petals, the shortest in length. This petal is shown in "4," as it looks when completed. For the next 8 petals, which are those of the medium length, the cup should come nearer the top, so the leaf would fall outward more, as in "5," and the last 5 petals, which are the longest. The crease goes clear through to the top of the petal in order that it may lie flat, and give the full blown effect as "6." Take a piece of stem wire the desired length, turn over its top with the pliers, making a loop that can be sewed through. Take 10 stamens, give them a twist in the center and double them and sew them firmly to the loop on the stem wire, as seen in "7." Wrap the first petal around the stem, as "9," and put on the second petal, as "11." The eight petals, which make the center of the rose, are arranged like this diagram:

The next eight petals are used in four groups of two petals each, which are sewed together at their base, slightly overlapping each other thus and each group overlapped in the same direction. These groups are arranged back of those in the center so as to alternate and not make straight lines of petals from the center to the outer edge, or to let them overlap like shingles as they go round the rose. The last five petals are used to fill in, where taste suggests, and they appear to be needed to fill out the perfect form of the rose.

Be careful in sewing on the petals that you do not get them farther and farther down the stem wire, thus making the center stand up too prominently. Some rose makers fasten the petals on with finest wire. I prefer millinery thread, as it is strong, and when used with the looped stem wire does not slip.

Now slip on the green cloth calyx on the stem wire. Frequently it is necessary to clip the calyx to make the opening larger, so it will go far enough up on the rose. Be careful and do not cut it so far that it can show above the seed pod, which is slipped on next. Arrange the calyx, so as to hide any stitching that may show on the base of the rose. Tack it in place with a fine needle and green thread, one small stitch to each section of the calyx and let it be near the stem.

Slip on the wax seed pod and wrap green thread around its base and stitch through the thread to keep the cup from slipping; place the foliage, letting its stems go with the stem wire into the rubber tubing. Give the stem the curve desired and your rose is finished.

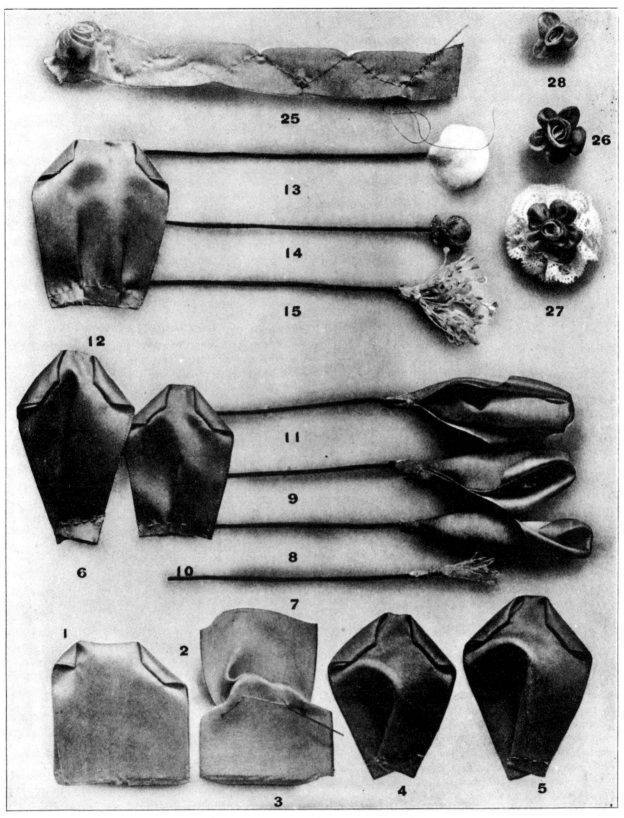

The Ribbon Rose from Stem to Petals.   Diminutive Decorative Roses

Figures 1 to 6 indicate how petals are prepared previous to being mounted on stems. Figures 1 to 11 demonstrate how roses B to G on page 13 are constructed. These, the stamens and arrangement of petals, are shown in Figures 7 to 15
Figures 25 to 28 picture tiny ornamental roses and their development

The Moss Rose Corsage Bouquet—(See F, Page 13)

It is made of No. 9 ribbon, of which it takes 2 yards. It really only takes 1 8/9 yards, but such fractions are not considered by the ordinary clerk. The petals are each 4 inches in length, 12 for the rose, and five for the bud. Those for the rose are all cupped in the center, as shown in figure "4," which gives it a half blown appearance. The petals for the bud have only one small straight crease, as "10," and are wrapped closely around the stem, which has a few stamens sewed to it as "8."

The moss calyx and stem are all in one, and slip up over the stem wire, and are secured by green thread, as in the cloth calyx. In the rose the stitching on the calyx is near the stem and in the bud half way up the calyx. The foliage is inserted in slits, cut in the stem sheath, and all wound tight with fine dark wire where the bud and rose stems cross. This is an exceptionally pretty corsage bouquet.

The Pink Cherokee Rose—(See C, Page 13)

This is an almost perfect reproduction of one of California's favorite climbers. Its flowers are pink or white. It clambers over fences, completely hiding them, or droops in long festoons from porch or lattice, and with its polished green leaves and myriad blossoms is a miracle of beauty.

It has five petals, each 3¾ inches in length requiring 18¾ inches for the rose. It is made of No. 12 ribbon. The rolls at the top are made smaller than in other roses and two small vertical creases are laid in the bottom of the petal, both in the same direction, as shown in figure "12." Gather the bottom in a slight arch in order to make the petal lie flat. Pull the gathering as tight as possible and sew it firmly. The stem wire is curved over with the pliers, wound with cotton as "13," covered with silk, sewed round in a circle as "14." I use changeable yellow and pink. The stamens are of varied lengths and many are used, as "15." Next the petals are sewed on just where the stamens are and are necessarily overlaid slightly. The under part and foliage are treated as in the full blown rose. The rubber tubing preferably has thorns on it.

The wild rose is made the same as the Cherokee, only of No. 9 ribbon, and only in pink or light dahlia red.

The Large Corsage Bouquet—(See G, Page 13)

These petals are made of No. 12 ribbon and each petal requires 5 inches in length; 12 petals for the larger rose, 7 for the smaller and 4 for the bud. This makes 3¼ yards of ribbon necessary. The cup in the petals of the roses, is in the center as "4," giving a half blown effect to the larger rose, and the petals of the smaller one are not creased over quite so much at the bottom, making them stand up a little straighter. The bud is made as the former one, as "10," anl "8." The rose is arranged with plentiful foliage, which is secured to the main stem wire, as are also the smaller rose and bud. The stem at its termination is short and covered with green tissue paper used in narrow strips. The foliage should then cover the stem, as the bouquet is so large; the stem is best out of sight.

In this instance the centers of the roses and all of the bud are made of ribbon, one shade darker than the outer petals of the roses—a few stamens in roses and bud improves them.

The Boutonniere Rose—(See D, Page 13)

The center is made of a bias piece of sheerest India silk doubled and made into a twist as "16." Four petals, with corners caught back, with one stitch and not rolled as "17," are given one crease in the bottom and grouped around the twisted center—a seed pod and small leaves are arranged tastefully. This makes a handsome effect on a gentleman's coat or for fancy trimmings for children's hats.

In making the twist of the silk, only curl it around once, and run the needle through and secure it, or you will make it too tight. It has to be loose to look well. Secure it to a turned-over stem wire.

Fabric Roses from Piece Goods—(See A, Page 13)

These are much cheaper than those made of ribbon, and can be made very decorative. Take the thinnest India silk, the 25 cents a yard kind. Cut bias strips, double them, cut off the desired length, and sew along the bottom in a curve, as "18." The petal will be more or less cupped, as you curve the gathering at the bottom, more or less. "19" shows the round petal. "20" shows the turned-back petal. The turn-back is on the underside of the leaf. "21" shows the folded petal, made as "22." "23" shows how to make the center of the rose, if you want a crinkly effect. It takes four petals to do this. "A" shows the completed rose, made of the different petals in piece goods.

The Tiny Roses—(See Page 9, Nos. 25 to 28

These can be made of ribbon or India silk. If of silk, cut a bias piece, double it, and make a twist for the center on one end and then sew out the strip as "25," which when drawn up tight will make five petals, which sew around the twisted center, and the completed rose will look like "26." It can be used for party dresses or children's caps when arranged as "27." A similar bud is made with three petals, as "28." Sometimes simple twists like "29" are used, with stem wire, seed cups and fine foliage, to good effect.

The small ribbon roses are made by cutting a bias piece like "30," doubling it and rolling it into a center like "31." Each petal, of which there are three, is made by taking exactly the same kind of a bias piece, doubling it, and sewing a gathering thread as "32" and drawing it up tight as "33." Sew the three petals made thus about the twisted center, and you have roses like "34" shown massed in the jabot. These roses can be used for any decorative purpose, but the base must be concealed, as it is very bulky. They are best in pastel colors, and used close together to hide the thick stem.

The Applied Rose—(See Page 12)

This is made of India silk on a round disk of buckram, padded on top with cotton. It is covered with a round piece of silk, gathered underneath. Bias folds are then laid across it and stitched in place, as "35." Four of these folds are gathered on the edge with very fine sewing, but only for the distance, not covered by the next fold. The foliage is made of a milliner's fold, which can readily be understood by looking at "35."

The applied rose featured in "35" is only one specimen of a variety practically unlimited. By varying the folds forming the foliage, charming festoon, trellis and garland effects may be attained, suitable, according to the size of the roses, for either hat or dress ornamentation.

Ornamental Flowers of Ribbon

Ribbon Snowball

Use narrow pale green and pure white satin ribbon. Make fewer of the green balls than of the white. Measure lengths of 18 inches; do not cut bolt until two or three blossoms are completed. These sections are made up into little loops, each 1½ inches long fastened with green-covered spool wire. The same wire forms 4-inch stems. Make up one bolt of these little bows, and group them to form snowballs. A full bunch of these is tied with No. 80 satin ribbon in same shade as green balls, with a full 6-loop bow, requiring about 5 yards of ribbon.

A Group of Decorative
Rose Bows

Ribbon Snowball

Single Rose and Bud

Use No. 30 white satin ribbon. For the bud double three inches of the ribbon and wrap about the wire in center of calyx. The rose is made of seven petals, varying between 1 and 1½ inches in depth, which are grouped about a bud. Finished with foliage and a single 2-looped bow with ends.

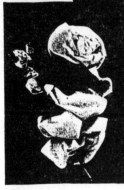

The Ribbon Calla Lily

Measure off a piece of bonnet wire and cover one end with yellow ribbon, winding about four inches in from the end. The remainder is wound with green satin ribbon No. 5, representing the stem. No. 80 white satin ribbon is required for each blossom. The ribbon is folded over, twisted about the stem and fastened with spool wire. The stem is wound last.

Violet Corsage

Ten yards of No. 1 violet satin ribbon are required to make this, with an additional half yard of baby velvet ribbon. Eight inches makes each little bow, representing the flower, and the ribbon is cut into these lengths.

Rose Buds and Rose Bows

Rosebuds and Rose Bows

To make ribbon roses, either cut the ribbon into lengths and form loops which are arranged about a rose center, or a wider ribbon is doubled and wrapped about a center. In the first case, several tones of ribbon may be used, simulating the natural shading. Use No. 40 ribbon in this instance. Full-blown roses are also made thus. Loops 2½ inches deep are gathered at the bottom and fastened to a stem with tie-wire. About 1¼ yards of ribbon is required when this method is employed as well as when the ribbon is loosely wound about a center. In this case wide ribbon is doubled, one end fastened to stem with wire, and the ribbon wrapped around it and likewise fastened with wire. The folded edge forms edge of petals.

Calla Lily

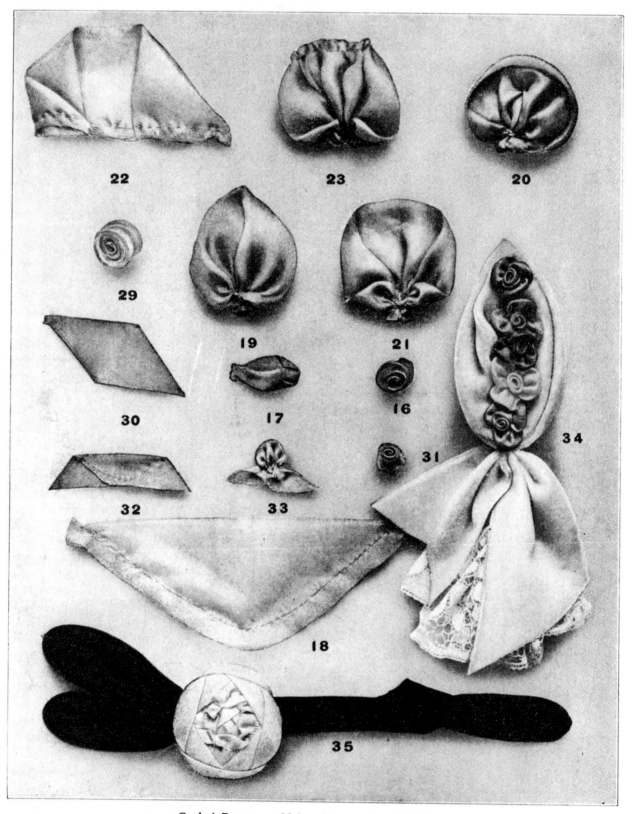

Gradual Progress of Making Petals and Applied Roses
(See Details, Page 10)

The manipulation of ribbon and piece goods in making rose petals is here demonstrated. Figure 34 illustrates a dainty rose-trimmed jabot; Figure 35 an applied rose with foliage

(See Instructions on Page 10)

Ornamental Roses and Corsage Bouquets

A. Fabric Rose	D. Boutonnière Bouquet of Rosebuds	B. Large Full-blown Rose
C. Cherokee Rose		E. Smaller Full-blown Rose
F. Corsage Bouquet of Moss Roses	(See Pages 8, 9, 10, 12 for Details)	G. Larger Corsage Bouquet

Lessons in Flower Making

This method of flower making is taught by Esther B. Lyon, of Pratt Institute, Brooklyn, also at University of Chicago Summer School

The first point in making any flower is to decide what type of stem the natural flower possesses, as all artificial flowers are built from the stem out. Choose from the Millinery wires the one that will best carry out the desired effect, as to size of natural stem and the general effect of the flower.

For example, the stem of a sweet-pea would suggest the green tie wire, which is the lightest weight wire used in flower making. The Chrysanthemum having by nature a firm stem requires the heaviest wire used in flower making, satin edge wire. The first point gained as to stem, the second step is choice of stamens. The Dennison flower supplies found in all large department stores carry a full line of stamens, as near the natural ones as may be found. Before securing stamens look at the natural flower to determine not only the type of stamens but the amount of stamens these flowers possess.

Third point is to tie with tie wire the stamens to the stems chosen.

Fourth step is to choose the color and width of ribbon best suited for copying the flower in hand. The cutting of petals of ribbon or velvet is next in order.

Fifth step, placing of petals on stem around stamens as the flower shows.

The last step is that of covering the stem so that the stitches in mounting petals are neatly finished; if the flower requires a great deal of sewing, a calyx is the best mode of covering stitches. This may be placed on the stem after winding the entire stem with green tissue paper.

This is an exact outline of the steps in all flower making. We will now go into the minute details as to each of the following flowers:

The Large Chrysanthemum—(See A, Page 16)

Cut stem 12 inches long, using satin edge wire if possible; if edge wire is not available frame wire may be used but not with as good results. First bend the end of wire over with wire cutters to form a small hook, place one bunch of rose stamens under loop of wire, tie securely with tie wire, press down with nippers. This makes a secure center on which to build your Chrysanthemum.

The Chrysanthemum takes one bolt of No. 3 satin ribbon. Cut ribbon in strips 5 inches in length, tie a knot in the center of each strip, as detail view on page 15 shows. Pleat the ribbon at base; sew together. It is easier to tie all the petals first, then pleat them, sewing with No. 5 Milliner's needles and 00 or medium fine Milliner's cotton. Next the petals are sewed on just where the stamens are and are necessarily overlaid slightly. Take great care in mounting petals as you sew round and round the stem that you do not run sewing down on the stem of flower so that the center petals will appear higher than the outer edge. To help overcome this difficulty the last row of petals around the outer edge of the Chrysanthemum should be cut one inch longer than the inside ones. The petals are now mounted on the stem. Cut strip of dark green tissue paper

two inches in width, long enough to wind around the entire stem, fold together double, paste at the top petals using millinery adhesive or library paste. To secure paper for a good start in winding, wind securely around stem as you near the end of stem, turn paper in and glue fast to wire for a perfect finish.

Pansies—(See B, Page 16)

The stems of pansies are made of green tie wire. This wire may be secured from Dennison flower supplies. Cut wire 8 inches long, loop over at end the same as Chrysanthemum stem. Tie a very few rose stamens with tie wire to stem.

The petals which are five in number are cut from scraps of velvet, using the pattern shown. Mirrored velvet is preferable as the shading light and dark best produce the shading of the natural pansy. After cutting the petals, a new point in flower making is necessary, that of wiring the petals without sewing. This is done by pasting the wire with Millinery adhesive to the back of the petals. Shape tie wire the exact shape of petal but enough smaller that the wire comes within 1/8 of an inch from edge, cover the wrong side of the velvet petal with Millinery adhesive,

PETAL FOR PANSY

Actual size of petal
Pattern for one petal

place the wire on side covered with glue. While the surface is damp, place a piece of silk or ribbon over this surface to line the petal, trim the lining with scissors after pasting to conform with the velvet on the outside. If a material is used which frays out a great deal a narrow binding should be used on the edge of petals and the tie wire may be run in the casing produced by the binding. The lining for the back may be slip-stitched on instead of pasted. This method should be used when scraps of silk delicate in texture are employed to carry out design, as pasting would stiffen the material.

After wiring and lining, the five petals are sewed on in the following order. The two upper petals first each overlapping nearly to the center of first petal, the side petals are put on alternately. The last petal making the lower edge of pansy is mounted on the outside of the others. Numbers show order in which petals are mounted. Finish stem with green paper same as Chrysanthemum. The centers of pansies may be touched up with water colors. A yellow pansy is very effective with dashes of black coming out of center.

Poppies—(See C, Page 16)

There are several ways of making poppies. The easiest way is cutting velvet petals from the pattern here supplied. Cut seven petals in all; the three inside ones, nearest the stamens are cut from the smaller pattern, the four outer

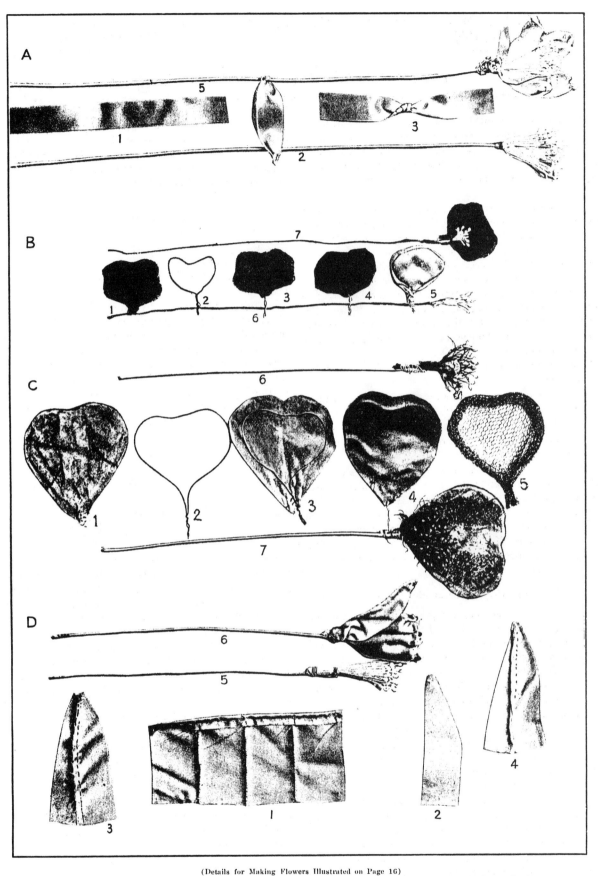

(Details for Making Flowers Illustrated on Page 16)

A.   The Ribbon Chrysanthemum from Stem to Petals

A.   Figures 1 to 3 indicate how petals are prepared previous to being mounted on stems. The stem, arrangement of stamens and petals are shown in figures 4 and 5.

B.   The Pansy from Stem to Petals

B.   Figures 1 to 5 show how petals are prepared before being mounted on stem. The stem, arrangement of stamens and petals are shown in figures 6 and 7.

C.   The Poppy from Stem to Petals

C.   Figures 1 to 5 indicate how petals are prepared previous to being mounted on stem. The stem, arrangement of stamens and petals is shown in figures 6 and 7.

D.   The Ribbon Jonquil from Stem to Petals

D.   Figure 1 shows cup-shaped center ready for joining in ring, with thread left open at top to draw up after placing around stamens. Figure 2 shows cutting of single petal. Figure 3 first seam run on right side and wire buttonholed to unfinished edge. Figure 4 shows finished petal with French seam. The stem, arrangement of stamens and petals are shown in figures 5 and 6.

Ornamental Flowers for Millinery and Decorative Purposes

A. Jonquil   D. Poppy   B   Chrysanthemum
C. Poppy   E   Pansies

(See Details on Page 15. Instructions for Making on Page 14)

petals from the larger one. Crimson velvet makes the most realistic poppies. After cutting the petals shape tie wire, the same line as finished petals, paste on back and line petal with same colored satin or taffeta. After making petals, before mounting touch up with water colors in center, mount around poppy stamens which have been tied onto a stem seven inches long, made of satin edge wire, finish stem of poppy with green tissue paper.

Poppies of Gold and Silver Cloth

Another way of making poppies of gold or silver cloth or beaded net is to cut petals after same pattern; finish edge with narrow binding cut from bias strip of material, turn binding in on wrong side and slip-stitch, thus finishing the

lighter shade than the center. These petals are cut from the pattern here shown. Dotted lines show depth of first seam and place to buttonhole tie wire on petal. The selvage edge of ribbons is placed on the straight edge of pattern, each petal is made up of two cuttings from the pattern. After cutting place the two curved edges together with the right side of the ribbon out, run a narrow seam as shown by dotted lines on pattern, button-hole tie wire to the unfinished edge of seam, run a second seam deep enough to encase wire and unfinished edge. In reality this is a French seam, the wire placed in after the first sewing. Make six of these petal mount around center, finish stem with green tissue paper.

These flowers may all be used for decorative purposes, as

LARGE PETAL FOR POPPY

PETAL FOR JONQUIL

SMALL PETAL FOR POPPY

petals without any lining. Tie wire is run in casing. Petals are mounted around stamens, five or seven petals may be used, an odd number of petals are best employed in any flower unless the natural flower calls for an even number.

Jonquils—(See D, Page 16)

Jonquils are slightly harder to make than the above mentioned flowers, but if each step is carried out carefully there will be no trouble.

A Jonquil like all flowers is built from the stem. First cut a piece of frame or hat wire 7 inches long, make a loop in the end of the wire, tie one-half of a bunch of rose stamens on the wire, mount the stamens on the wire as high as possible so they will come near the top of the cup-shaped center which is to be made of ribbon. Ribbon in two shades of yellow is used in making jonquils, the cup-shaped center is darker than the outer petals. For this center ¼ yard of No. 5 ribbon cut in four equal parts, making the strips 2¼ inches in length, turn strips on the wrong side and sew over and over joining each strip onto the other, the selvage edges placed together. The last sewing joins the ribbon in a ring. Turn down the top of ribbon ¼ of an inch, shir ⅛ of an inch from edge, leaving the thread used for shirring unfastened at top, slip the ribbon center over the stamens, pull thread up until the ribbon touches the stamens at top, pleat the lower edge and sew to stem. The outer petals are six in number and require one yard of No. 5 ribbon of a

well as for millinery trimming. Artificial foliage for all flowers can be obtained cheaper than it can be made, and is available almost everywhere that millinery is sold.

Lily of White English Crape

A splendid suggestion for trimming millinery for second period of mourning. Each petal has a fine wire foundation, over which the crape is draped in the manner illustrated. The center is formed by a tiny chou of black satin, crepe or any other desired material.

Cockades and Motifs of Ribbon

The cockade or rosette of ribbon is a perennial favorite because it can be varied in countless different ways giving the milliner every opportunity of displaying her ingenuity.

The uncommonly smart and jaunty designs illustrated are all of the tailored variety, suitable to be used on street and semi-dressy millinery of all descriptions.

center in the manner pictured making six loops. Finish these carefully, fasten at center and arrange ends as in illustration. One yard of ribbon is allowed.

Maltese Cross

Again No. 5 grosgrain ribbon may be used, making eight clusters of three plaits each, about 8 inches deep. Then fold

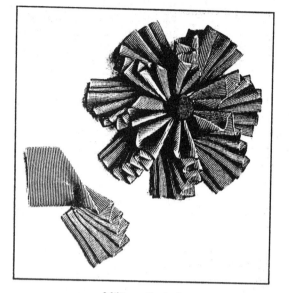

Military Cockade

The cleverly conceived Military Cockade is made of 1 1/16 yards of No. 5 grosgrain ribbon, and consists of seven sections: three straight plaits succeeded by four slanting plaits, all fastened to a buckram foundation, and finished with a small button. The detail view shows how the folds are arranged.

Maltese Cross

back corners and tack as in illustration. Join all at center to a buckram foundation, and finish with a folded square. Two and one-sixteenth yards are required for making this motif.

Propeller Motif

This can be used as a cockade or fancy tailored bow effect. Use No. 5 grosgrain ribbon making two clusters

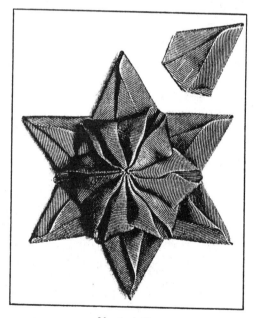

Nautical Star

This design is made of No. 5 grosgrain ribbon, and features six points fastened to the edge of a buckram disk. The ornament may be made in any desired size, this one being about 3½ inches across. The ribbon is folded at the

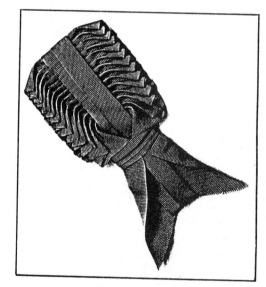

Propeller Motif

of side plaits, about ⅜-inch lap, fourteen plaits in each section, then join together at center, leaving ends to slash when finished. Now tack carefully corners of plaits, as in illustration, fold ribbon and draw over from end to end. A folded strap of ribbon clasps the center.

Ribbon Motifs

Wing Motif

Suggestion for a small tailored effect. May be employed in many ways. It is made of two-toned moiré grosgrain ribbon No. 5, tied in four flat knots and joined together to overlap. Fasten securely on buckram foundation. One yard of ribbon allowed.

Legion d'honneur

An ultra-smart motif developed of No. 3 grosgrain ribbon. Plait up one yard, forming small side plaits about one and one-eighth inches deep. Now join three lengths of ribbon and bind the edge, drawing center length to center of ornament where a small covered button flying three streamers with slashed ends is secured as a finish.

Wing Motif

Legion d'honneur

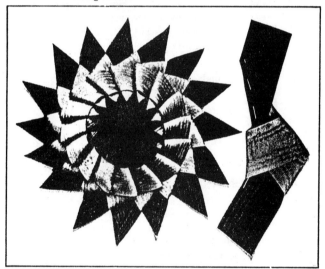

Buzz Saw

Pin Wheel

Form a buckram cone same as in No. 5 and follow the same method, making sections by folding instead of tying knots (see illustration), then sew the twenty-two sections to buckram foundation.

At first glance this motif appears intricate, but in reality this, as well as the Pin Wheel, are simple to make. Begin by forming a buckram cone, cutting out a circle the desired size, then slash to center, lap over and fasten. In this ornament No. 5 two-toned moiré ribbon is employed. Form sixteen sections by tying flat knots as illustrated and folding one end over a little. Now carefully sew all to the buckram cone foundation, taking care to lap all ends neatly at center, after which all outside ends are slashed as shown in illustration. This motif is also very effective in a solid color. Four yards of ribbon required.

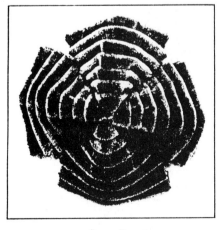

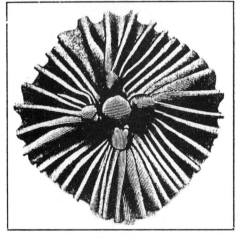

Cross Rosette

A very effective motif developed from No. 9-12 velvet ribbon. Form two sections of fourteen tucks about one-quarter inch deep, and close enough together to hide stitching. Now fold seven tucks each way and fold ribbon at center. Make both sections alike and join spreading ends as in illustration. One yard of ribbon required.

Tall Three-Loop Bow

Useful for imparting height to small hats

Cocarde

Formed of No. 5 grosgrain ribbon, side plaited about one quarter inch in depth (three-quarters yard, plaited and joined in circle). Bind inner edge with ribbon and arrange in four loops or sections which are drawn up so as to leave loops to stand around a small ribbon-covered button, as in the finished ornament. One yard allowed.

Ribbon Ornaments for Hat and Dress Trimming

(See Illustrations on page 21)

No. 1—Toy Top Motif

Ornament No. 1 is made from No. 16 satin ribbon (a good quality of grosgrain also looks well). Begin by folding ribbon as shown in No. 2, continue until 36 points are formed, then with needle and double thread catch all together in three places as shown and knot together firmly; having done this, one readily can see how to make the remaining finish by drawing all the loops around to form a circle. Now twist a piece of lace wire and secure to one end and you have a very smart ornament to stand out from crown or edge of brim.

No. 3—Ribbon Sunburst

The smart rosette pictured in No. 3 is formed of No. 16 satin ribbon; No. 4 shows method of making folds. These must be held in place, as we proceed, by tacking with needle and thread until we have secured 16 points at center and 32 points at back; then with needle and double thread secure all the loops firmly as in figure No. 4, and arrange in circle, being careful to finish remaining edges neatly. This makes a very handsome trim for a side crown, using one in front and one at back on small turban effect or narrow brim sailor.

No. 5—Dahlia Rosette

The single Dahlia Rosette shown in No. 5 can be made from wide ribbon or a piece of satin or silk. To form this rosette ten pieces of material 5½ inches square are used. Take two pieces, lay right sides of material together and stitch all around, then make small opening in one piece only and turn—this leaves all corners and edges perfect. The ten pieces will make five finished squares. Now look at figure 6 and fold squares accordingly, leaving opening inside when folding, and with thread and needle tack it lightly as shown. When all five are ready, fold the long points together leaving short points on outside, when you will readily see the next step, which is to join all five together in a circle. Bear in mind that you must be governed in regard to size of this rosette by place you wish it to occupy. It is very pleasing when made much smaller, in which case several rosettes are applied around crown to simulate flowers.

No. 7—Pinwheel Rosette

In the Pinwheel Rosette we may again use wide ribbon or piece goods may be used. This time 16 pieces 5½ inches square are needed. Proceed as for No. 5 rosette and when turned and ready notice No. 8, fold all squares thus and run heavy thread through center as shown, fasten tightly together and proceed to spread out flat, when you will at once secure the outside effect, then by carefully folding back each corner around center you will have completed the ornament, which may be used similarly to suggestion for No. 5, or in many other ways, by forming this of smaller squares and joining two rosettes together back to back and wiring, an unusually smart trim may be effected to stand up from crown or out.

No. 9—A Conventional Rosette

This motif is excellent for severely tailored side crown, placing several of them close together as the only trimming on a smart tailored shape. These can be formed of two materials as illustrated or developed in one solid material and color. Once more we use two squares, this time half of different sizes to allow for covering wooden molds; these can be obtained at any large department store;

the one used here is about one inch in height and nearly round, with small hole through the center. The back of the rosette is formed of two squares 5½ inches, joined and turned as before, the remaining one being 6½ inches square. Now with needle and thread catch center of square and pull through mold, slightly hold and fasten them, gathering all the fulness around mold and fasten securely at back, then spread out flat and even fulness and fold over sides as seen in rosette. Then tack firmly to center of back square again, folding corners of same as in illustration.

No. 10—Rose Motifs

Very effective when made of two materials in two tones. This makes a beautiful design to use flat on upper brims or around side crowns and in various other ways. The models here used are in graduated sizes of circles stitched double and turned as before described, one 4-inch circle, one 3½-inch circle and one 3-inch circle, laid one upon another and tacked at center. The final one that completes the flower is 3½ inches, which by being drawn partially over a small wooden button mold allows enough fulness and is tacked in place last. By the addition of foliage as suggested in illustration a more elaborate effect is obtained.

No. 11—Flat Cabbage Rose

Another conventional flower effect made in the same way, using the one-inch round wooden mold for the center. Measurements used here are: back circle, 4 inches; circle to cover mold, 5½ inches.

No. 12—Morning Glory Motif

No. 5 heavy corded ribbon is used 3¾ yards being allowed. From light weight buckram cut a circle 3¾ inches in diameter, inside mark out circle 1¾ inches and cut out carefully; now take a small piece of buckram and fold into funnel shape just large enough to slip through the opening and extend 22¼ inches, cut balance away, allowing funnel to slip through circle easily; now fasten one end of the ribbon at small end and holding both pieces lightly but firmly with the fingers of the left hand, proceed to weave ribbon over and under, repeating operation until the form is entirely covered. By wiring edge of ornament with lace wire same will now easily hold in shape when finished with four or five sections to simulate a morning glory. This makes a decidedly novel as well as practical ornament to be fastened at a tangent on the crown.

No. 13—Spool Motif

Very clever ornament for smart turban or hat with rolled brim. No. 5 heavy corded ribbon is again used. Cut from light weight buckram a circle 4¾ inches in diameter, mark circle in center 2½ inches and cut out, then slash outer edge and lap over ⅓ of circumference and join firmly; form two such concave circles and holding same together as shown in illustration, fasten end of ribbon and again with right hand weave the ribbon over and under until form has been closely covered, then fasten and twist ribbon lightly and draw through center over outside and finish when same is joined to hat with small bow as suggested in illustration. You will notice that this description applies to a perfectly circular ornament, whereas the one illustrated is somewhat oval; one can obtain this effect easily by cutting an oval and lapping same as described for circle. This ornament can be placed directly on top center of crown of small cap effect turban to very good advantage, or in any other preferred style.

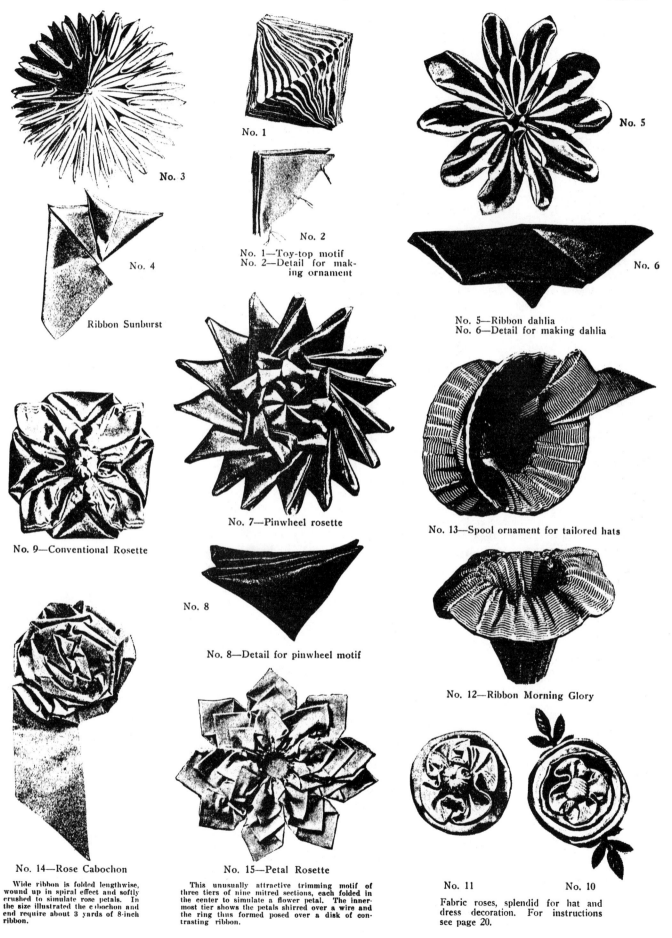

No. 3

No. 4

Ribbon Sunburst

No. 1

No. 2

No. 1—Toy-top motif
No. 2—Detail for making ornament

No. 5

No. 6

No. 5—Ribbon dahlia
No. 6—Detail for making dahlia

No. 9—Conventional Rosette

No. 7—Pinwheel rosette

No. 8

No. 8—Detail for pinwheel motif

No. 13—Spool ornament for tailored hats

No. 12—Ribbon Morning Glory

No. 14—Rose Cabochon

Wide ribbon is folded lengthwise, wound up in spiral effect and softly crushed to simulate rose petals. In the size illustrated the cabochon and end require about 3 yards of 8-inch ribbon.

No. 15—Petal Rosette

This unusually attractive trimming motif of three tiers of nine mitred sections, each folded in the center to simulate a flower petal. The innermost tier shows the petals shirred over a wire and the ring thus formed posed over a disk of contrasting ribbon.

No. 11   No. 10

Fabric roses, splendid for hat and dress decoration. For instructions see page 20.

New and Smart Ribbon Motifs

(See opposite page for Illustrations)

No. 1—Ornament

This ornament cannot do itself justice by illustration as it depends largely upon its placement on the hat for its beauty, when it fully justifies the effort required. To form same, six finished 6-inch squares are required, and again the contrast of color adds to the effect; begin by folding cornerwise and placing one on another; join carefully, leaving open space in center; now spread out one end and join the other end, bringing all six points close together as seen in illustration.

No. 2—Cone Motif

This ornament is made by first forming a cone of buckram the desired size, leaving small opening at the top; begin by taking ¾-inch ribbon and form a knot; fasten to the extreme outside edge of cone, lap end over and fasten; now take up to center and pull through small opening and fasten; repeat this operation, each time allowing the knot to lap about half way over the former one, and continue until entire cone has been covered. You will find the result a very pleasing ornament, at once suggesting a smart trimming.

No. 3—The Cocarde

The cocarde, a very smart trimming motif, may be used in various ways, as a trimming for a sailor or walking hat. It requires 1½ yards of ¾-inch ribbon. Form four clusters of two loops each, folding tightly together and join firmly at the base, allowing ends to fall together and slash as shown; finish by folding ribbon twice around to cover joining and finish neatly at the back.

No. 4—Daisy Motif

This unique motif is formed like in the cocarde, using eight clusters of two loops each with slashed ends. All are joined securely at center, where ribbon is bound around and knotted, leaving ends slashed to match ends of loops; 2½ yards of ¾-inch ribbon required.

No. 5—Cabochon

Another similar ornament, a little more complex in appearance but equally simple in arrangement. Begin by forming buckram cone of desired size and cutting off about halfway up, leaving a large opening at center. Now take ¾-inch ribbon and fold one-third over and lightly press with hot iron; then follow same instructions as for No. 8 ornament until entire cone is covered, having fastened each short end at back of cone; now whirl the long ends together and slide through large opening and fasten.

No. 6—Decorative Buckle

Handsome buckle, made by following the same method as of the flat knot, each folding about halfway over the former. Cut buckle pattern first the desired size; have the ¾-inch ribbon folded and lightly pressed as for ornament No. 9 and make a flat knob and fasten at center, then carry ribbon back of pattern and twist once, bringing around to top or front of buckle and continue until pattern is covered.

The amount of ribbon required will of course depend upon the size of buckle.

No. 7—Conventional Rosette

This effective design requires four pieces of material six inches square, joined and turned as already described and laid crosswise of each other, drawn carefully over large button mould, and about 1½ inches across; after fastening lay out flat and tack all corners back as seen in illustration; the finish around button is effected by cutting crosswise a small strip of tucked material of contrasting color; form into a small roll and fasten carefully just at back edge of button. This may be omitted, but only at a sacrifice of the beauty of the rosette.

No. 8—Cross Motif

Simple but effective arrangement of ribbon in the form of a cross, excellent as a trimming for severely tailored models, may be used flat on upper brim or side crown with equally pleasing results. It is hardly necessary to explain the method of forming this ornament, as it is so simple, being four groups of folded graduated points, the last one having ends slashed, and finally all four groups are fixed at center by stitching securely to a buckram foundation, after which the buckram foundation is trimmed away.

No. 9—Fruit Bud Ornament

Novel ornament simulating fruit bud, made in contrasting colors and arranged with foliage, will be found very effective. This requires two 6-inch circles of material joined and turned; make small opening in one and turn; this leaves a perfect edge. Now take a piece of cotton wadding or soft mull, and form a round mould about 1¾ inches in diameter, and with a heavy thread gather all around edge about ⅜ of an inch from the edge and draw up around mould and fasten. Then arrange fulness of the gathered edge into conventional center as shown in illustration.

No. 10—Ornamental Pin Motif

Ornament which may be used to very good effect as an ornamental pin. Cut two pieces of material six inches square, pin and turn as before described, then with cotton or mull form round mould about 1¾ inches in diameter, now run gathering in circular form about ⅜ inches from sides of square, draw up carefully around mould and fasten, then arrange ends together as seen in illustration, when an ordinary hat pin may be inserted and fastened. Then the ornament is ready for use; made in contrasting colors adds to the effectiveness.

An Effective Way of Braiding Ribbon

A novel feature and a smart trimming is that of covering a hat crown with a checker board pattern of interwoven fancy ribbon with contrasting metallic edge. There are fourteen of these ribbon strips (the length to be determined by the size of the crown) and the ends are taken together on each side to form a sort of fan, which produces an uncommonly pleasing effect on a dark foundation.

New and Smart
Ribbon Motifs

(See opposite page for descriptions)

No. 1—Ornament

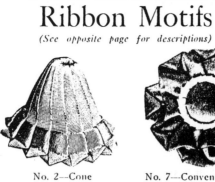

No. 2—Cone

No. 7—Conventional Rosette

No. 8—Cross Motif

No. 5—Cabochon

No. 11

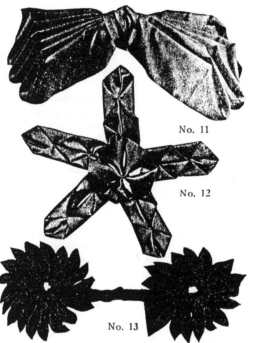

No. 12

No. 13

No. 9—Fruit Bud
Ornament

No. 10—Ornamental
Pin Motif

No. 6—Decorative Buckle

No. 11.   Triple Alsatian Bow, with crushed and folded-in loops.

No. 12.   Star motif. Consists of five wired section, covered with cleverly folded satin ribbon, and finished with a five-point center.

No. 13.   Twin Dahlia Rosette. Each flower form consists of 18 petals, joined to a wire ring at the base. A knotted ribbon strap connects both motifs.

No. 14—Loop Cluster

A clever application of
the Cocarde

No. 3—Cocarde

No. 4—Daisy Motif

Chic use of the Daisy
Motif

Large and Small Bows of Ribbon

(See page 25 for Illustrations)

Trimming motifs made of ribbon are always in season and always prove splendid sellers. While all kinds of ribbons are used to some extent, preference is as a rule given to medium widths which are particularly desirable for making into clever rosettes and ornaments suited for trimming tailored millinery.

Outside of flowers, which thanks to their endless variety, allow of innumerable combinations of form and color and an infinite variety of arrangement, ribbon is the most important factor in the line of trimmings, affording a particularly wide scope to the ingenuity of the designer.

Poinsettia motif made of heavy satin, grosgrain or faille ribbon, with ribbon-covered button molds forming centers.

Rose Cross

A very effective ornament, so called on account of its resemblance to a cross made of rose petals. To form this, 3½ yards of No. 16 satin ribbon is used.

First fold over ribbon making one loop 3¼ inches in length, repeat three times making each following loop ½ inch shorter. Then with needle threaded catch the corner of each loop and fold under and tack as seen in illustration. Next boxplait the three loops together at lower end and fasten securely. Make in all four groups and join together forming a cross. Then fasten end of remaining piece of ribbon at back and bring over and across twice, softly folding; fasten at back.

Coquette Bow

A simple but very pretty bow for which 2½ yards of No. 9 satin ribbon is needed. Begin by folding over seven loops each about ¼ inches shorter than the preceding one and slip between the fingers as you would unfold a fan and with needle and thread tack carefully between the loops. Then lay in one side-plait and fasten securely. Repeat this operation and form the two groups (as shown in illustration). Use two widths the proper length, folded and then turned back to form keeper or waist of bow.

Passion Flower Motif

Two and one-half to two and three-fourths yards of No. 7 ribbon are necessary. The quantity depends upon the number of petals desired. By careful study of the illustration which shows each step taken to form the petal, one petal may be made. The operation is repeated until the desired number is obtained. One should have a needle threaded and catch the ends as ribbon is folded, and finally draw the thread up very tightly and fasten, being careful to finish the ends, so as to form the last petal. A small covered button or tiny tailored bow may be used to further ornament the center, or it may be left as in illustration.

Crescent Bow

Three yards of 5-inch ribbon are required for making the entire bow, 1½ yards to make each crescent loop. These are made by shirring one inch from the outer edge, also run a ⅜-inch tuck on the inner edge. Through the outer edge lace wire is drawn, while the inner edge is stiffened with brace wire. Form wired ribbon into crescents. The remainder of the ribbon is used for making four loops, two 9, the other 6 inches long, which are connected by a soft center knot and drawn through the crescent motifs.

Buckle Bow

The Buckle Bow is made similar to the bow just described, but all of the loops are left straight, none of the corners being turned over and tacked. This bow is made quite elaborate by the addition of an oval buckle motif, which is wound with narrower ribbon, the center filled in with a crushed puff of the wide ribbon. This bow may serve a variety of purposes, being equally effective when finishing the girdle of a dress as when adorning the crown or brim of a hat.

Fancy Alsatian Bow

This bow is made of 2 1/6 yards of 4½-inch ribbon, and consists of two 8-inch loops, two 6-inch loops, two 4-inch loops and one 2-inch loop. Three inches are counted for the knot. Tack the corner of each loop as illustrated.

Large and Small Bows

Rose Cross

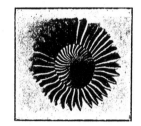

Passion Flower Motif

Coquette Bow

The Rose Cross an all-sufficient trimming

Detail showing how loops of Passion Flower Motif are mitred

The Passion Flower Motif used in conjunction with quills.

Crescent Bow

Buckle Bow

One way of using the Crescent Bow

The Buckle Bow used as crown trimming on a broad-brimmed hat.

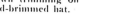

Fancy Alsatian Bow

Ribbon Flowers and Bows

Rosette Bow

Two yards of No. 100 ribbon are required for developing this novelty bow. Four loops wired at each edge with ribbon wire form the upper part of the bow; two of them are twisted to form a stick-up, while the other two are folded in the center to make two extra loops. The base is made of 1 yard of ribbon cut through the center to form a shirred tuck in which wire is inserted, making four additional loops.

Aeroplane Bow

For making this effective bow three yards of No. 100 ribbon is required. The center is formed by seven loops, wired along one edge, and the pleasing arrangement is completed by an 8-inch wire rod wound with ribbon, and finished at either end with two small, unwired loops of the ribbon.

yards of ribbon. The rose is made of one continuous strip wound in spiral effect and tacked to place, and it is supported by a stem wound with frayed green ribbon and finished with sprays of foliage. A double hanging loop of the ribbon topped by a soft twist finishes the base of the stem.

Dahlia Bow

For each dahlia take ¾ yard of No. 100 ribbon. Crease ribbon into 2-inch folds, shirr along creases, fasten to wire and cover the stem thus formed with ribbon in the natural shade of green. The bouquet illustrated herewith may be employed for various decorative purposes, while the dahlias, separated, make a very attractive garniture for hats.

Inverted Pyramid Motif

Make three loops of 8-inch ribbon, the first 11, the next

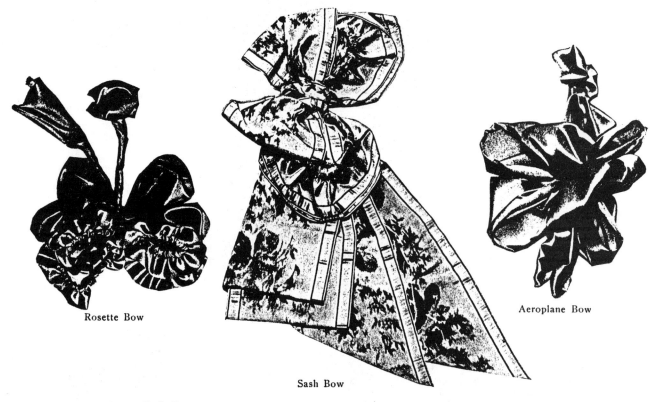

Rosette Bow

Sash Bow

Aeroplane Bow

Sash Bow

Three yards of ribbon required. Make two long loops, one of which is 1 inch shorter than the other two, two short loops equally long, and two long ends. The remainder is tucked through middle length and drawn into open loops by means of wire or cord.

Ribbon Hops on Rod Stem

Made of No. 100 ribbon, of which 1½ yards is required. One yard of the ribbon is shirred every two inches across the width of the ribbon; draw up the thread and fasten to the wire rod, which is wrapped with the remainder of the ribbon. The hops hang loosely from the top of the stem; the base is decorated with a little rose of the ribbon.

Rose Stick-Up

This highly ornamental trimming motif requires 2½

9 and the third 7 inches long; turn the outer edge of the upper part of each loop to center front and the lower edge back. Use ½ yard of ribbon to make the rose, the center of which is finished with three ribbon-wound antennae. Two-inch strips of the ribbon are shirred about the base, which is finished with an end made of ¼ yard of ribbon cut diagonally and laid in pleats below the shirring. Only the longest loop is stiffened with wire.

Foliage Bow

This is a particularly decorative ribbon arrangement, splendidly suitable for hat trimming. It requires 5 yards of No. 100 satin ribbon, formed into twenty-one 7-inch loops. The remainder is used for forming the two ends. The loops are fastened to a strip of ribbon wire covered with ribbon.

No more graceful back trimming than the Foliage Bow.

Foliage Bow

Inverted Pyramid Motif

An effective garniture employing the Inverted Pyramid Motif

Dahlia Bow

Ribbon Hops

Ribbon Hops a fascinating substitute for tassels

The Ribbon Rose Stick-up trimming a portrait hat

Ribbon Rose Stick-up

Machine-Sewed Bows
The Sewing Machine as a Time-Saver

The advantage of employing the sewing machine in making trimming bows in quantities is easily recognized. This procedure will prove particularly helpful in cases where bows are made in quantities.

No. 1—The Triple Dahlia

Made of No. 100 ribbon, requires four yards, cut into sixteen-inch lengths. One end is folded back and hemmed a width of one and one-quarter inches; one-half inch from this row of machine stitching, another tuck or loop an inch and one-fourth long is made; one-half inch from this second row of machine stitching a very small tuck is run in on the upper side of the ribbon; one-half inch from this small tuck another loop one and one-quarter inches is put in, then another one-half inch from this last row of machine stitching is made a narrow one-quarter inch hem. These three side tucks and two small ones consume the sixteen inches of the ribbon. Eight other pieces of ribbon are made up in exactly the same manner. All this work is done on a sewing machine. The shirring wire is run through the last or top tuck and drawn tightly together into a ring not more than one inch in diameter. A shirring wire is then run through the narrow tuck which is just between the one single side tuck and the double tucks at the end of the ribbon, and this wire is drawn into a circle three inches in diameter. Twist the ends of the wire together and pull each of the nine loops in position and the rosette is finished.

No. 2—The Meteor Bow

This bow requires 3 yards of No. 100 ribbon. Fold the ribbon in the middle with the face inside. Place the center of the fold upon a strip of ribbon wire. Sew the ribbon by machine to this wire. Open the ribbon so that the face side is cut and the ribbon wire is concealed in the center of the loop. Make the loop of ribbon nine inches long, that is, use eighteen inches of ribbon folded back so that the loop will be nine inches long and gather at the bottom and wrap securely with a heavy thread. Measure from the bottom two inches and make another nine-inch loop. Again measure two inches and another nine-inch loop. The balance of the ribbon, which has been wired, is wound around the base of the third loop, is then carried to the second loop and wound around the base of this one. Then on to the first loop and in like manner. After this the ribbon is twisted and placed just back of the three loops and wound round and round in a widening circle until the base bow is properly formed. Each time the ribbon is wound around it is poked through the knot which formed the base of the last loop. The different two ropes of the ribbon must then be tacked to the side loops. This bow is probably best adapted to the trimming of large or medium hats on the right side of the crown. As many loops may be made as desired, according to the proportion of the brim upon which it is to be placed.

No. 3—Fancy Loop Bow

Cut a strip of ribbon one yard in length, fold in the middle and draw the two ends to overlap one another at the center of the bow. Cut the next strip thirty-two inches long, fold and loop together in same manner as first piece of ribbon. Cut the third strip twenty-eight inches long, the fourth strip twenty-four inches long, and the fifth strip twenty inches long. Fold each one the same as No. 1. Lay them together, each strip of ribbon slightly overlapping the other. Sew them together with three rows of stitching. This is better shown by Bow No. 4. The center of Bow No. 3 is made by using Bow No. 20 which is described further on.

No. 4—Drooping Loop Bow

The same as No. 3 with the exception that the loops on both sides are allowed to fall down. This bow is particularly well adapted for back trimming.

No. 5—Chrysanthemum Bow

Requires four yards of ribbon. Run narrow hem at the ends of No. 100 ribbon. Use a tape measure or rule, or a five-inch length of cardboard and make a small mark every five inches near the edge of the ribbon until twenty-six loops are thus marked off. Fold satin-faced ribbon together at the first five-inch mark and run in a narrow tuck on the sewing-machine on the reverse of the ribbon. Now on to the next mark and put another tuck. Continue this, taking each five-inch mark until the twenty-six tucks are made. Run a shirring wire through from right to left through the first tuck, then run it through the second tuck and each tuck successively, being careful to start the wire at the right and run through to the left. Shove these tucks closely together and tie the wire into a five-inch circle. Thread a needle with silk thread the same color as the ribbon and push together; when all the twenty-six have been strung tie the two ends of the thread together.

No. 6—Wreath Ring Bow

Identically the same as No. 5 with the exception that it is left open in the center. This arrangement of the ribbon is best used around the bottom of bouquets of flowers, clusters of feathers or circular cabochons, placed in the center of the wire ring.

No. 7—Beetle Bow

Requires four yards of No. 100 ribbon. Take a twelve-inch strip, fold the ribbon back, and sew straight across on the machine. This makes a six-inch loop. Measure one inch from the end of this loop and put in another six-inch loop. One inch from the bottom of this loop put in another six-inch loop, and one inch further on, another. Measure off one yard of ribbon, and at the end of the yard put in four more six-inch loops, being careful that they are exactly one inch apart at the bottom. This completes the two ends of the bow. Put seven or nine narrow tucks in the yard length. Be sure that the tucks are on the outside or rather satin-finished side. Run a fine shirring wire through each tuck. Push this ribbon together on the wires with the top wires drawn shorter and tighter than the bottom edge. Draw this shirred portion around and tie in a knot. Now take each loop separately and pull the two top edges inside of center and tack securely or sew on a sewing-machine

Machine Sewed Bows

(See page 28)

No. 1—Triple Dahlia

No. 5—Chrysanthemum

No. 3—Fancy Loop Bow

No. 2—Meteor

No. 4—Drooping Loop Bow

Cataract Bow

A decorative flat arrangement of loops, made of one continuous length of ribbon. The loops are folded in the manner illustrated, turned over in the center, and held in place by two rows of machine stitching.

No. 7—Beetle Bow

No. 6—Wreath Bow

for one-half inch. This produces the double-pointed effect on each loop.

No. 8—Star Bow

Eight yards of ribbon are required for this bow. Twenty-seven pointed loops are cut. Each end of each loop strip is folded back to meet the selvedge edge of the ribbon.

No. 8—Star Bow

This produces a triangle of ribbon. The two edges of the long side of the triangle are folded in to meet in the middle. Three separate rows of these loops overlapping one another are sewed on to a strip of ribbon about one and one-fourth yards in length or about as much as all nine loops will

No. 9—Flower Bow

cover placed side by side. The inner edge of this band of ribbon has a small hem through which a small wire is run and drawn tightly to the center.

No. 9—Flower Bow

The loops of No. 9 are made the same as No. 8 with the exception that fourteen loops are used and these are strung on a wire which is drawn to a ring with a diameter

of one and one-half inches. A piece of the same width ribbon is wrapped over this wire between each loop. Three or four of these bows can be mixed with foliage forming an entire trimming for a large hat.

No. 10—Flat Bow

Bow No. 10 is made the same as Bow No. 15. It is merely the band folded back to form a quill effect.

No. 10—Flat Bow

No. 11—Ear of Corn Bow

No. 11 is made identically the same as No. 8 with the exception that the ribbon after being finished in the band is wrapped around a stick, which is then withdrawn and produces the ear of corn design.

No. 11—Ear of Corn

No. 12—Crown Garnitures

Crown garniture shows the fancy band No. 15 drawn to a circle to be used around the crown of a hat and is then finished at the side with a rosette bow of the same ribbon.

No. 14—Erect Bow

Three yards of ribbon are required for this quill. The ribbon has a small tuck through the center beginning four inches from one end and going the entire length of the ribbon. This strip is then pushed tightly on a five-inch length of wire. The other two strips are treated in a like manner. The ends of the ribbon are then placed together, the wires being tied at the top and also the bottom. The ruffles should be pulled apart in order to produce a fluffy and rounded appearance.

No. 15—Fancy Band

A fancy band of folded ribbon woven back and forth and double sewed with a double row of stitching near the edge. This design may be used on waists, or skirts or as fancy garnitures in a variety of forms. It is shown as a quill in No. 10 and as a hat band in No. 12.

No. 12—Crown Garniture

No. 16—Petal Band

A band of ribbon which may be used for flounces on skirts or trimming for other garments. It is made for millinery in No. 8 and as an ear of corn in No. 11.

No. 17—Aster Bow

Each loop of this rounded bow is made by hand, each one separate from the other. After the required number of loops have been made, the first and last are joined together, leaving an opening at the center. Through this the end of the ribbon is pulled and wrapped between each loop,

No. 17—Aster Bow

forming a very solid center. The band that accompanies a bow of this sort is made of No. 60 ribbon folded in the center with the satin side out and is then crocheted by the finger and not with a hook in a band sufficiently long to reach around the crown of a hat. One must have an understanding of crochet work in order to make this a success.

No. 18—Hanging Loop Band

This is simply a different arrangement of pendant loops as shown by bows, Nos. 3 and 4.

No. 16—Petal Band

No. 14—Erect Bow

No. 15—Fancy Band

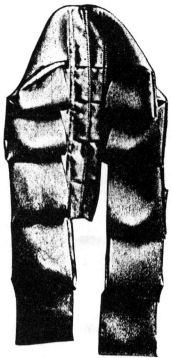

No. 18—Hanging Loop Band

No. 19—Cluster Bow

This bow requires ten yards of No. 16 satin-faced ribbon. Take a piece of cardboard six inches in length and make a mark on one edge of the selvedge every six inches the entire length. Dirctly in the center of this space, equidistant, from both marks, tie a knot. After the entire ten yards have been tied in the knots of which there will be about sixty, the ribbon is folded together, the satin face in at each place where the small mark was made. Sew narrow tucks on the sewing machine. After this is done, thread

No. 19—Cluster Bow

a tape needle with baby ribbon covered with the same ribbon. Begin at the bottom and sew these loops separately to the buckram, going around and around, gradually filling in to the center. Bows of this order should be used three or four of different colors on a hat.

No. 20—The Double Ring

This bow requires two yards of ribbon: two hems and three tucks are made in this entire length. These tucks are made to show underneath. Fine wires are run through these hems and tucks, after which the ribbon is shoved close to the end, and fashioned into a knot as shown in the illustration. The same bow or knot may be worn on a girdle for a dress, and is used as the center of the trimming band pictured in No. 3.

No. 20—Double Ring

No. 21—Cockade

This smart bow is made of narrow ribbon, knife or side plaited on the sewing machine. Attach first to the outer edge of the buckram piece, gradually filling in to the center.

No. 21—Cockade

No. 22—Band Trimming

No. 40 ribbon folded back and forth diagonally, held in place by pins until the left hand row of stitching is first put in. Remove all the pins and start with the bottom loop, pulling it back. Pull the second, third and other loops back in the same manner and pin in position after which run in the right hand row of stitching. This peculiar folded-back arrangement produces the raised center.

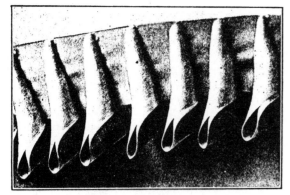

No. 22—Band Trimming

No. 23—Step Band

A finished band trimming to be used around the crown of hats, the edges of gowns and garments. Lay the ribbon flat on a board, fold as if to make a loop, take the upper left-hand corner of what would naturally be the extreme edge of the loop and push it down inside until the folded center comes even with the selvage edge. Pin in position, and make second or succeeding loops in the same manner, carefully pinning each one separately. After the strip has been finished, place this selvage edge under the foot of the sewing machine and sew firmly.

No. 24—Plaited Band

A simple, plain band trimming for hats, made of three strips of ribbon, plaited together in exactly the same manner as you plait the hair.

No. 25—Rosette Bow

Each loop or petal of this rosette bow is cut bias at both ends. However, the bias points of each end run in opposite directions. The outer edge of the selvage is about seven inches long while the inner edge is less than three. By turning the pattern end for end each time, not a particle of the ribbon is wasted. Attach a shirrer to your sewing machine and shirr every loop. This may be done in one continuous string, after which it is attached to the buckram cabochon form beginning at the outer edge and working to the center.

No. 25—Rosette Bow

No. 26—Zigzag Band

A piece of ribbon, No. 22 in width, is simply folded back and forth, the points of one loop overlapping the other and held in place with a pin. After the required length has thus been made, two rows of machine stitching hold the different loops in their respective positions.

No. 27—Crochet Band

For the crocheted band No. 27, make the five-inch strip into a loop which will be two and one-half inches long and sew straight across the ribbon on the sewing machine. Beginning at the next mark which is one inch further on, fold the five-inch strip into another loop and sew on the machine. Continue this until the band of sufficient length is then made into numerous loops. Take each loop separately and curl under, pull down and tack through the back of the band with thread in same color as ribbon. Little bands of this kind are very chic on hats for misses and also for skirt trimmings.

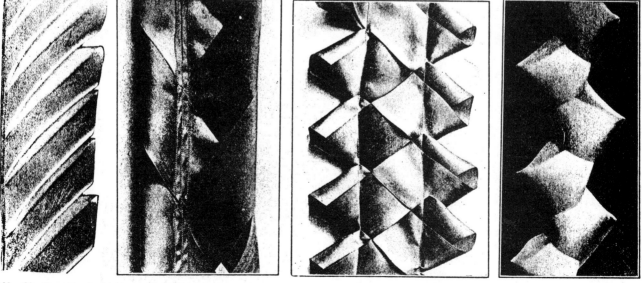

No. 23—Step Band   No. 24—Plaited Band   No. 26—Zig Zag Band   No 27—Crochet Band

No. 28—Butterfly Bow

The Butterfly Bow requires about six yards of ribbon. Narrow tucks are put on the wrong side of the ribbon about five inches apart, through which the narrow lace wire is drawn. Pulling the wire taut causes the ribbon to circle and curl around this wire producing a sausage effect of the ribbon. The small loop is made for the top then drawn through the fingers; a loop is made for the bottom, drawing the ribbon again through the hand; the outside loop which encircles upper or top loop lying directly on both sides of the first small loop produces the head of the butterfly. The ribbon is then drawn around the longer or bottom loop which produces the body. Grasp the ribbon sausage in the right hand and lap it round and round to form the upper portion of the body as shown in illustration. The wings are made by sewing four strips of the ribbon together on a sewing machine in the center of this wide band, or in other words, sewing from side to side. Run five small tucks, the tucks to be on the upper side of the ribbon. Through these tucks run a tape measure drawing a double string of spool

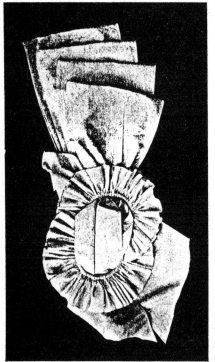

Wing Bow

A smart and uncommonly ornamental decoration for hat or dress sash. Consists of four loops of graduated lengths and three ends which are drawn through a buckle slide of frilled narrow ribbon shirred to a wire form.

wire. Pull same closely together so that the space will not be more than two inches long of the shirred piece. Sew this on the back of the butterfly and trim both the edges in the form of the wings of the butterfly.

No. 29—Quill Bow

This bow to be used standing high on either side of the hat is best produced and most effective if made in three or more colors. Lay six strips of ribbon, each cut 12 inches in length on top of one another. Cut the top ends pointed all at the same time. Begin with the top layer of the ribbon and slide it down about one-quarter inch. The second one the same, the third and so on, until the back strip extends about one-quarter inch above the one next to it. With this arrangement cut in a point the bottom, sew with a sewing machine in the middle of the six pieces of ribbon, running the same near the top, turning it and following down, leav-

ing a small space about one-quarter inch wide between the seams so that the wire may be pushed up between the third and fourth layer of the ribbon. Take the bottom points and lay the top fold of each over and near the center. The second piece of ribbon is brought up in the same manner, leaving space of about one-quarter inch. The third, fourth, fifth and sixth pieces are treated in a like manner. A sewing-machine then is used to fan these corners and hold them securely. A circular bow is placed at the bottom and secured to the upright bow. This bow is now ready for being adjusted on hat.

No. 30—Roll Bow

The ribbon is tucked about 5 inches apart through which the lace wire is drawn from left to right and right to left after which the wire is drawn taut causing the ribbon to roll entirely around the wire. Grasp the end of the ribbon in the left hand and make loops of suitable length, going first to the top then to the bottom and back to the top and again to the bottom and so on until the required number of loops have been finished. Draw the end of the ribbon tightly around the center and fasten it back with a needle and thread.

No. 31—The Mitred Loop Motif

The flat motif shown under No. 31 is not only very stylish, but one of the most economical designs to be obtained. The loops are shallow, being double only half their apparent depth. For instance, the first loop is four inches deep. Upon this another is made two inches deep and pinned to place as shown in the right hand figure of the second illustration. Marking with a pin two inches beyond this loop on the ribbon, third 2-inch loop is made, and so on, until the series is complete.

After pinning the loops they are tacked in with needle and thread. A length of ribbon is extended ten inches and tied in a knot finished with pointed end, or a second series of loops is made when a double bow is required.

When a flat bow will not fill the requirements of the trim the same bow is treated as shown in the illustration. The ribbon is turned in at each side and a pointed loop results, which gives a bow of quite different character, but equally as smart as the flat bow.

To the Bow Maker

It is hardly necessary to remind the bow maker that new ideas in bows are to be observed, studied and applied from season to season. A gift for making graceful bows, like other talents, must be cultivated before the possessor becomes a full fledged adept in the art of handling ribbons. This book places before the expert the newest conceits in ribbon for copy and suggestion, and aids the adept and the novice by directions, measurements and comments.

Methods of Practice

Where bow making presents difficulties it is a good idea to practice with cheap materials, cut into strips, to represent ribbon. Cambric is about the best material for this purpose. Old or faded ribbons may be used, the same piece serving for many of the tied bows which are made up without cutting the ribbon.

One of the first essentials to success is the ability to handle ribbons daintily, without creasing or mussing them. A clear conception of the bow in mind makes the way easy for the maker. In many instances it is necessary to cut the ribbon into lengths to make a successful bow, and in many others cutting would prove a detriment, in some cases a positive ruin of the bow to be made.

The Butterfly Bow, a suitable decoration
for broad brimmed hats

No. 32—Ribbon Chou

Four-inch ribbon is used for
developing this effective ornament, whose size depends on the
number of (crushed) loops one
chooses. Suitable for millinery
and dress trimming.

No. 28—Butterfly Bow

The Quill Bow makes a fascinating
trimming for berettas

No. 29—Quill Bow

No. 31—The Mitred Loop Motif

No. 30—Roll Bow

Machine Made Ribbon Rosettes

By means of narrower ribbons than are ordinarily used, the handsome rosettes illustrated here are made. They are all made of ribbons four inches wide. They are large and showy and designed for millinery. The small designs made of narrower ribbon will make rosettes smaller but equally effective where small ones are needed. When narrower ribbons are used, loops are shortened to preserve the same relation of length to width which is shown in these illustrations.

No. 1—*The Pine Cone Rosette*

This bow consists of four long loops and one end, each 14 inches in length. That is, a length of 28 inches is required for each loop. These loops are laid in the ribbon without cutting it, and five casings for small wires—shirring wires—are made by machine stitching across the ribbon at the center. In these casings shirring wires are inserted and the ribbon fulled on the wire. The shirring wires are from 7 to 9 inches in length. The ribbon is tacked at the end of each shirring to place, and the band of shirrings thus

crowded on it, is sewed to a foundation disc of buckram, three inches in diameter.

No. 4—*The Flower Rosette*

A clever rosette consisting of 14 loops, 5 inches deep, and an end. The loops are sewed to a buckram foundation, which is covered with a bit of ribbon and a circle of wire wound into ribbon. A ribbon 4 inches wide is used for this rosette, although it can be made in either wide or narrow numbers.

No. 5—*Sun-Flower Rosette*

This rosette is made of petals of ribbon sewed to a buckram disc which is 3 inches in diameter and bound with small bonnet wire at the edge. Four-inch ribbon is used for this rosette which will be either larger or smaller as the ribbon is wider or narrower. At intervals of 11 inches strong shirring threads are run across the ribbon and this is gathered as full as possible at these points to form the large petals. There are ten of these and they are sewed to the

The Pine Cone Rosette trimming edge of a brim revers

No. 1—The Pine Cone Rosette

Flower Rosette trimming a portrait hat

made joined by sewing its edges together at the back of the bow. When the band is completed in this manner twist the bow giving the loops the diagonal direction shown in the illustration.

No. 2—*Daisy Rosette*

Rosette made of satin ribbon, four inches wide, consisting of thirteen loops. These loops are made from lengths of ribbon, the allowance being sixteen to eighteen inches. These lengths are folded under at one end to a depth of about five inches, and at the other to a depth of about three inches, there being a little variation to produce variety in loops. Two shirring threads are run at the base of each longer loop, forming a casing for a small wire. The shirrings are one-eighth inch apart. Twelve inches of wire is allowed, overlapping one-inch at the end.

One inch from these shirrings a second shirring is run with two shirring threads. The thread runs diagonally across the shorter loop, forming a series of points in the center of this rosette. Half the points are left upstanding and half are sewed down to the center. The rosette is finished with four pointed ends, two eleven inches long, one ten inches and one 3½ inches in length.

No. 3—*Carnation Rosette*

This rosette is made of lengths of ribbon trimmed into fishtail points at both ends. Eight inches are allowed for each length. These lengths are folded at the center over wire, to which they are sewed. A bolt of ribbon is consumed in making this rosette. The wire having the ribbon

buckram with the extra fulness (formed by tacking them to the edge of the buckram disc) caught to the foundation also.

Smaller petals are made by cutting the ribbon to half its width. That is, it is folded lengthwise, and cut along the fold. It is then formed into petals in the same manner as those for the larger petals, or the half widths are cut into four-inch lengths. These lengths are gathered at each end and folded into the petal form shown in the picture. They are then sewed to the foundation.

No. 6—*The Windmill Rosette*

An economical rosette made of four-inch satin ribbon is shown here. It consists of eleven hems hemmed 1½ inches deep and having a tuck 1¼ inches wide, overlapping the hem ⅛ inch. These ends are eight inches long when hemmed and tucked. The ends are shirred on a wire which is four inches long, overlapping ¼ inch to form a circle.

No. 7—*Chrysanthemum Rosette*

This rosette is made by hemming the ribbon on the machine, along one edge, in a hem ⅛ inch wide. A fine shirring wire is run in the hem. The ribbon is then made into 12 loops, each one knotted at the center. Fifteen inches are allowed to make each loop. These loops are sewed to a disc of buckram at the center, three inches in diameter. This foundation is covered with fifteen small puffs. These puffs are made of the ribbon laid in a lengthwise pleat and sewed in short loops, gathered at their bases. A length of 3½ inches is allowed for each puff.

Rosette Ornaments for Various Decorative Purposes

Daisy Rosettes make pleasing garnitures for Sports millinery

No. 6—Windmill Rosette

No. 2—Daisy Rosette

No. 3—Carnation Rosette

No. 4—Flower Rosette

The Flower Rosette (No. 4) applied

No. 5—Sunflower Rosette

No. 7—Chrysanthemum Rosette

No. 8—Rose Bow

This is a flat rose bow having three ends, 7, 9 and 10½ inches in length respectively.

A bit of crinoline 4 inches square is folded into a foundation to support the bud or folded petal at the center. To cover this, a 5-inch length of the ribbon is folded lengthwise, and folded over the foundation and sewed at its base. This is sewed to a foundation of buckram which is a disc 3 inches in diameter.

The remainder of the rose is made by sewing the ribbon along one edge to the foundation, laying it in irregular pleats to form the necessary fulness. A portion of the edge is turned back at intervals to simulate the curl in a natural petal. When the rose is completed a loop 4½ inches deep is sewed to the buckram completing a very handsome decoration. Rose color, pink, dark red or any of the colors in which roses grow, should be chosen for this bow.

No. 9—Aztec Step Bow

This simple arrangement of flat loops is useful for the back or side of many hats and may also be shirred where the machine stitching appears. It consists simply of ten 10-inch loops. They are arranged in the manner shown in the illustration, and basted to a strip of paper. After this a triple row of machine stitching is run along the basting in parallel rows, something less than ¼ inch apart.

No. 10—Checker Board Bow

This bow, a new form of the basket bow, consists of four loops, each 8 inches deep, and 4 loops from 14 to 10 inches deep, finished with two pointed ends, each 7½ inches long.

Ribbon from No. 60 to 100 may be used for this bow, the narrow number is shown in the illustration. It is hemmed along one edge on the machine and a tiny shirring wire is run in the hem. The ribbon, thus prepared, is laid in the longer loops, allowing for one of the long ends an additional length of 3½ inches.

Begin the crosswise shorter loops by allowing the additional 3½ inches for the second end and weave the ribbon over and under the first loops, crushing it to occupy space about an inch in width. Continue to weave the ribbon in this way until the bow is completed, tacking the weave to place with needle and thread. This is an elegant decoration for millinery.

The rose bow on this page is intended to be mounted flat against the hat or garment it decorates. It is a model which can be copied in ribbons of narrower widths and put to many uses. Made of inch-wide ribbon with little roses, makes a lovely decoration for elaborate gowns, and similar tiny roses of No. 2 ribbon are most elegant for fancy work.

Simpler flower forms, such as the daisy and forget-me-not, can be made of baby ribbon and used instead of embroidery for decorating all manner of dainty fancy articles for personal use and for household articles. The most beautiful examples of this work are to be found in France, and a little study of the opera bags, toilette cases, etc., made by the French will reveal the possibilities of ribbons in this direction. Medallion frames, in which the opening for a picture is outlined with a wreath of tiny ribbon flowers are also very attractive.

No. 11—Tie Bow

This simple arrangement of ribbon is useful for ties and sashes. It consists of four loops, 5, 6, 7 and 8 inches deep, respectively, with the loops wound with tie wire at the base and covered with a very tight double knot from which the long end is suspended. Velvet ribbon or silk ribbon 3 inches wide will make a tie like that shown in the picture.

No. 12—Seven End Tie Bow

Consists of a series of flat loops tacked together at their bases and tied in a braid knot with a pointed end finishing the group. The loops are turned in at each side and the edges tacked together, giving the pointed effect shown in the illustration.

No. 13—Cogwheel Bow

This odd rosette is made on a foundation and is only practical for millinery. It consists of eighteen loops and one long end which will form a single tie or streamer. It is made of 4-inch ribbon. The loops are 4 inches deep and folded into a point at the ends of each length of ribbon. These points are tacked together with needle and thread. The loop is then doubled lengthwise. The sides are then folded down, the points all turning the same way. At the end of the folded end portion the loops are sewed together at the center.

No. 14—Pompon Bow

A simple rosette made of 4-inch ribbon consists of 18 short loops each 4 inches deep, gathered at their bases and sewed together forming a pompon of loops from which a long end is suspended.

One must consider in the selection of ribbon the use to which it is to be put in connection with the weave, finish, lustre and its "body" or weight. Taking the ribbon pieces shown on this page, for example, ribbons of various character of weave and finish, lustre and body are employed to make them successfully. For the tie shown in Fig. 11 one would select a ribbon having considerable body, and either a high or soft lustre. Faille ribbon would be a satisfactory weave for this piece. In No. 12 one might use faille, but messaline would prove as successful, and in some instances a better choice. For the novel motif shown in Fig. 13 a ribbon having considerable body is necessary. The design is too elaborate for a ribbon of light weight, and much of its beauty would be lost if the lustre were not high. A heavy lustrous taffeta, a moiré or a satin ribbon of sufficient body would prove the proper selection for this number. For Fig. 14 a soft and light weave is to be chosen. Such ribbons are not "mussable," if we may use the term, and can be easily ironed out. Wide ribbons in the most pliable or simplest varieties turned out by the looms are suitable for sashes whatever their weight, so long as they are not flimsy.

In this connection it may be remarked that the manufacturers, to meet the advance in public taste, are able to turn out ribbons of finer appearance for less money than ever before in the history of the industry. Colorings are also better than in former years. In ribbons, as in other merchandise, very good looking, indeed beautiful, effects are turned out that are within the reach of everyone.

No. 15—The Utility Bow

A bow of seven loops and two ends. Four, five and seven-inch loops, an end five inches, and one seven inches long make up the bow. It is made on the fingers by means of the wire, which is wound about the base of each loop,

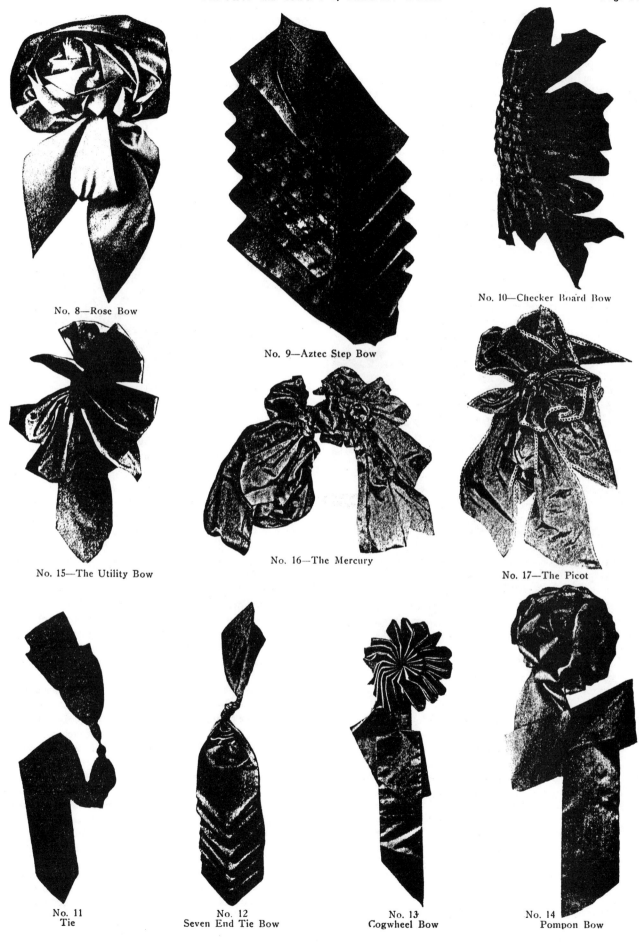

No. 8—Rose Bow

No. 9—Aztec Step Bow

No. 10—Checker Board Bow

No. 15—The Utility Bow

No. 16—The Mercury

No. 17—The Picot

No. 11
Tie

No. 12
Seven End Tie Bow

No. 13
Cogwheel Bow

No. 14
Pompon Bow

after allowing a length for the shorter end, two inches longer than in the finished bow. After tying all the loops with tie wire the ribbon is brought around the center of the bow and tied in a firm knot. Two and a quarter yards are required for this pretty and sprightly bow, which is made of wide taffeta ribbon, a No. 80 in this instance.

No. 17—*The Picot*

This represents a bow made of wide novelty ribbon, with a fancy edge. No. 100 ribbon is selected. The bow consists of three ends, four loops and a ruffle of the ribbon, tied with a tight knot at the heart of the bow. The two long ends are twelve and fourteen inches in length, the shorter ones seven and eight inches. The loops are six inches in depth, requiring twelve inches each; three-quarters of a yard are allowed for the ruffle. The bow is made with needle and thread.

No. 16—*The Mercury*

This view represents a bow called the Mercury, from its resemblance to a pair of wings. It consists of five loops on each side and a center of short loops or puffs of ribbon.

Double Rosette with Bud

The loops vary in size from four inches to ten inches in depth and one side contains an end ten inches long with pointed end. Each side contains one loop ten inches long, one eight inches, two six inches and one five inches long, making in all seventy inches or two yards lacking two inches. Allowing ten inches for the extra end, six inches for five small loops or puffs and the tie, it will require five yards of No. 80 ribbon for the bow.

The multitude of ways in which these bows may be used make them particularly valuable to the trimmer. They permit the use of left-over pieces of ribbons.

Double Rosette with Bud

Two rosettes, made of taffeta ribbon, Nos. 80 or 100, are joined by means of a band of the ribbon and form an excellent trim, especially for a child's hat. The ribbon is hemmed and wired with a very small wire on one edge,

although the rosettes may be effectively made without wire. Each rosette has eight loops, four and a half inches long.

Ribbon Plume

The ribbon plume is made for under trimming of brim, requiring five yards of soft No. 40 satin ribbon.

The arrangement of the loops is quite simple. A loop five and a half inches deep is fastened to a wire stem to form the tip of the plume. Six loops at either side, each five inches deep, are fastened to either side the wire stem by means of tie wire. These loops are placed in a slanting direction as shown in the illustration. A quill end finishes

Ribbon Plume Trimming

the plume at the base, being thrust over the ends of a folded loop of ribbon which covers the wire rib of the plume.

A variation of this plume may be made by knotting the ribbon on the wire rib. Long ribs of metal, plain or set with stones, make an elegant finish. By making the loops shorter very handsome ribbon quills are formed. These latter are excellent decorations for smart street hats.

Bow of Crushed Ribbon

A chic hat garniture is made of very wide ribbon. A rosette of four short loops is joined by the ribbon, twisted to a wide bow. This bow consists of seven loops graduating in length and tied at the middle. The bow terminates in a bias end tied in a knot. The garniture is meant to form the entire trimming for a large, soft hat, such as are worn by misses and children. Lustrous ribbons are the only kind suitable for this bow, the crushing bringing out tones in the lights and shadows that are very rich and pleasing to the eye. The effect would be lost in a ribbon of ordinary sheen.

We should handle ribbons as we do flowers—carefully, for like flowers, they are sensitive to the touch and often suffer greatly when handled by someone who does not know or appreciate their delicate texture. We should always keep in mind when forming a bow to keep it looking fresh and crisp as a new blown rose, therein lies the beauty —shall we say art—of creating a bow; the same is assuredly true with regard to ornaments of any character made from ribbon, they should have all the appearance of having bloomed without requiring the assistance of needle, thread or fingers.

Beautiful ribbon bows and ornaments are as much the expression of a beautiful thought as is some wonderful strain of music, both proceed from the same source, and express to a greater or less degree some attribute of the beautiful.

For Corsage and Sash

Bows for the corsage require soft, supple ribbons that lend themselves to the full crushable bows used in the present mode. Sash bows and sashes, on the other hand, require ribbons of considerable body. Many a simple costume is quite transformed by the addition of handsome garnitures of this kind. They are particularly pretty with light summer gowns, for dinner gowns and for evening wear.

Quite intricate is the corsage bow shown in Figure 1 (Matinée). It consists of three ends and three series of loops

The Matinee

than four pieces, however, to make it, as the long ends, loops and short loops, are made in one piece each. A length is allowed for the two short ends with an additional allowance of six inches for the knot. This length is tied tightly about the base of the short upstanding loops and completes the design. Seven yards are required to make the bow shown of a 4½ inch or somewhat wider ribbon. The long ends require a yard each, the long loops three-fourths and the short loop one-fourth yard each. One yard is allowed for the short ends. This makes a very full bow. Less ribbon is required in wider numbers, as only two long ends are then necessary.

The Opera

A full sash bow of wide figured sash ribbon consists of three long loops, four short ones and

The Matron

The Opera

with a fulled ruffle or "drape" of ribbon introduced among the bows. The ends are respectively sixteen, twelve and eight inches in length. The first series of loops are eight inches in depth, the second five and the third three. This is a sewed bow. The loops are caught with needle and thread at their base, with a short length of ribbon caught about the center or waist of the bow. The two shorter ends are then tacked in the bow. In addition to the ribbon measured off for the long end, about a half yard is fulled by being gathered on one edge and cascaded into the bow among the loops. Such an arrangement of loops, ends and cascaded ribbon consumes six yards of No. 60 or 80 ribbon, the wider number being usually chosen.

The Matron

Figure 2 shows a simple bow and sash ends made of Dresden ribbon with bordered edges. Three long and two short pointed ends, with three long and three short loops make up the garniture. In the illustration the long ends are folded in order to show the pointed cut. This is a sewed bow. It is not necessary to cut the ribbon into more

two ends, one of which is long. When very wide ribbon is used the sash is made with two hanging loops and ends. The ribbon is not cut for this bow. After measuring off sufficient lengths for the long end the loops are made and sewed at the base. After making in this way all the loops, the ribbon is brought then about the waist of the bow, the short lengths slipped under the ribbon thus drawn about, and tacked with an invisible stitch. The long ends require a yard, the loops respectively 54, 36, 27 inches. The short loops require nine inches each. Fourteen inches are allowed to wrap about the waist and make the short end.

Striped ribbon in an attractive color combination may be substituted for the figured effect; or a sash ribbon in a solid color with fancy edge or metallic selvage may be chosen, if rich simplicity is desired. There are practically no limits to the successful development of this bow.

Millinery Bows

Fleur-de-lys Bow

This bow requires three yards of No. 100 ribbon, cut into six one-half yard lengths. Five of these lengths form the petals of the bow. The raw edge at the ends of each piece is turned down to one edge of the ribbon, and the whole plaited in together and tied securely with the wire. Having formed the five petals in this way, three are arranged to stand upright and two downward. The remaining half-yard piece is used to make the knot and a half-blown petal. Measure off half its length for the knot and place a pin to mark this length. Make a small petal of one-half this length, as before, and twist the remaining half about the bow to form the knot. Thrust the small petal up through the knot.

Two shades of ribbon may be used for this bow, and if a heavy quality of ribbon is not obtainable a lighter quality may be used, but will require wiring.

A pretty variation of this bow may be made by first plaiting the ribbon. Ribbon with sufficient body should be selected to keep its shape, as this is more satisfactory in this or any other bow than wiring. Made of narrower ribbon, this bow makes a handsome corsage garniture. Of wide ribbon it is suitable for sash bow as well as hat trimming. It is a stylish and always fashionable bow, adapted to plain or figured ribbons.

When made of wide ribbon for hat trimming, it will be necessary to support the loops with ribbon wire.

The Ladder Bow

This bow requires three and one-half yards of No. 30 ribbon. The ribbon may be wired with a flat wire, which is placed up the center with invisible stitches. The loops on the left-hand side are about four inches deep. Four of the loops on the right-hand side are each five inches deep. The one long loop is seven and one-half inches deep. This allows a remainder of thirty-one inches for the five knots and one pointed end. Begin at one end of the ribbon, forming the lowest loops first. The loop on the left-hand side is made, then the opposite one on the right-hand side. These are sewed firmly, or can be fastened securely by winding with tie wire. Then throw the piece of ribbon over the center and bring the end up through from underneath. You now have two loops and one knot. An inch from this knot begin to form another left-side loop, then a right-hand one, and then the knot. Continue this, observing dimensions as given, until bow is completed.

The Dragon Fly Bow

This bow requires three and a quarter yards of ribbon to make. It is adapted to children's hats especially, and to any wide brimmed, picturesque shapes. It consists of four long loops, each one-quarter of a yard in length. The ribbon is folded along the middle and caught with a few "blind stitches," as shown in the illustration. Five small

loops form the center, in place of the usual knot. An end of ribbon finished with two small loops and a sharp end completes this particularly good and always fashionable bow.

Spider Bow

This bow is not essentially new, but it has proved such an attractive trimming that a collection of bows is not complete without including the spider bow. The spider bow is often made of black velvet ribbon. However, the model for illustration was fashioned of No. 5 pearl white

The Spider Bow

satin ribbon. It took four and one-half yards to make this bow. The ribbon is hemmed at one side and fine wire run through. Loops of various sizes are made and then bent into bow knot effect.

The Poinsettia Bow—(See Page 45)

This bow of velvet ribbon consists of four or more loops, varying from three to five inches in length. These are wired with small silk-covered wire, tacked to the back of the loops. It is much used, especially as a decoration in connection with flowers for hats with upturned back brims. In this case the bow is tacked to the back bandeau and the loops spread to lie against the hat and hair. The wire used must be very small, otherwise the effect will not be graceful. It is easy to estimate the amount of ribbon required for this bow. Allow 8½ inches of ribbon for each loop, but in making up the loops vary the length; that is, allow 8 inches or a trifle less for some and with a trifle more for others.

Butterfly Bow—(See Page 45)

This bow requires two and one-half yards of wide ribbon to make. It will be found necessary to hem and wire one edge unless the ribbon is of an unusually heavy or stiff body. Both ends are trimmed to a point, and may be tucked as shown in illustration.

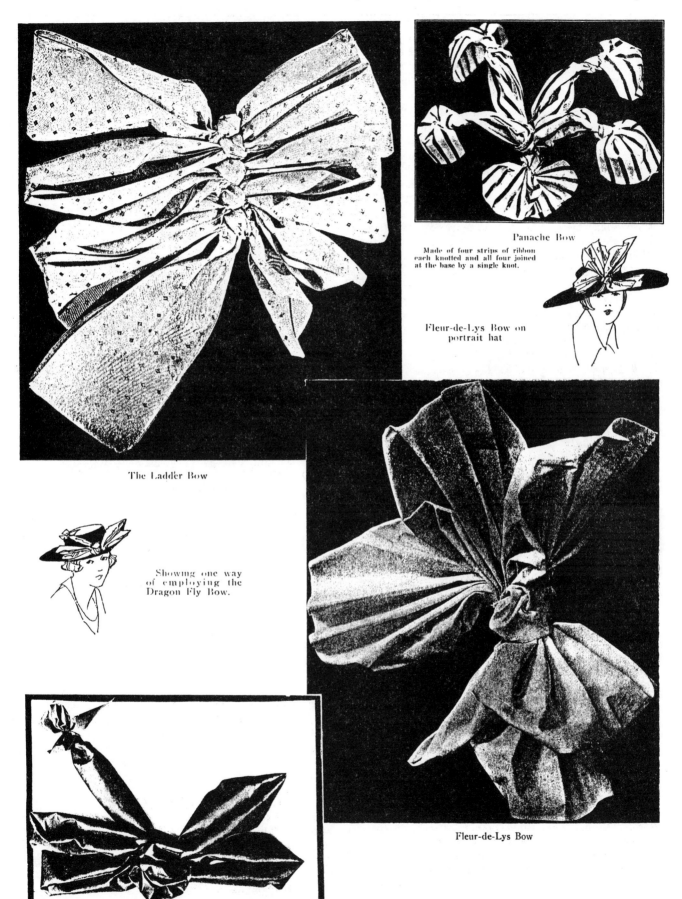

The Ladder Bow

Panache Bow

Made of four strips of ribbon each knotted and all four joined at the base by a single knot.

Fleur-de-Lys Bow on portrait hat

Showing one way of employing the Dragon Fly Bow.

Fleur-de-Lys Bow

The Dragon Fly Bow

The ends are each nine inches long, as are also the two longest loops. The shorter loops are seven and one-half inches long. This bow is made with tie wire. The base of the first point end is pleated in and tied with wire, or, rather, wound with wire. The loops are then made, being wound at their base with tie wire. They are disposed— one of each length—at either side, simulating the wings of a butterfly. The remaining end is tied in a double knot about the center of the bow with the pointed end arranged to stand as shown in the picture. This bow is very popular in all the medium and wide ribbons, and is equally suitable for dress or hat garniture. It is an excellent sash bow.

Diamond Bow

This strikingly clever bow requires four yards of No. 40 ribbon. The original model was of liberty satin of pretty sheen and fine texture. The first step in making the bow is to wire two yards of the ribbon with a pliable wire, by running in a hem at the side. The slashed ends of ribbon are not wired, only the loops. The unique appearance of the loops is due to a peculiar arrangement of the ribbon. The loops are made as follows: Take two yards of wired

Diamond Bow

ribbon, measure off two spaces of sixteen inches, another of fourteen inches, and the last about twelve inches. Place pins at each of these points. Now fold over the ribbon lengthwise along the center, thus bringing the selvage and wired edge together. Find the exact center of each loop to be; that is, find the point that will be at the top of the loop. On each side of this measure an inch and a half, then at these points sew the two edges together. Now the diamonds are formed by opening these sewed spaces, bending the ribbon at the point where pin was placed to mark the exact center, so that the wired edge is bent upward and the selvage is brought down. Now form the loop as in an ordinary bow and a diamond shape will come at the top of it. After making each loop the rest of the work is comparatively easy. Cut short pieces of ribbon, slash the ends and bunch together. Sew these to the group of loops. An end of ribbon is left of the wired two yards. Twist this

around in a knot, standing the tall pointed end among the loops.

Fancy Knotted Bow

It is best, when making this bow, to wire with flat ribbon wire, sewing with invisible stitches up the center of the ribbon. The ribbon is then slightly coiled or twisted and then tied in loose round knots. The model bow required

Fancy Knotted Bow

four and one-half yards of No. 40 ribbon. One of the loops should be six inches high, another seven inches, and still another five and one-half inches tall. Pointed ends are left after tying a pretty knot.

The Wheel Bow
This Bow is not Illustrated

To make this ribbon trimming it will be necessary to have about nine yards of ribbon, No. 30 being a good width. The side bow consists of ten loops, five inches deep, using up ten inches of ribbon in each loop. Wrap each loop separately with tie wire, then make a series of side crown bows, which should consist of three loops of the same length, without a center, and fastened to the side crown of the hat. After a sufficient number of bows have been made they should be attached to the hat, either six or eight being used for one hat, and placed either two or three inches apart midway in the center of the side crown. Twist a piece of straight ribbon very tight and fasten one end securely under the round side bow. Carry the ribbon to the first three loop bow and twist around the base, causing it to stand out from the side of the hat. Continue this process about each bow, and after each bow has been thus wrapped, the end is carried to the side and hidden underneath the loops.

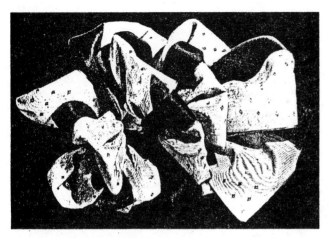

The Pyramid Bow

Double Knot Bow

Pyramid Bow

To make this handsome bow a wide ribbon must be used of sufficient "body" or stiffness to hold position without wiring. Bow consists of a series of loops, two at the top, each about four inches tall (using eight inches of ribbon for each loop). Then make four loops about three and one-half inches deep. Then tie a knot of the ribbon about the wire. The remainder of the loops are three and three and one-half inches deep. About two and three-quarter yards of ribbon make a pretty bow of this kind.

Cascade Rosette

Four yards of five-inch ribbon are required to make this intricate rosette in a size large enough to cover the crown of a hat. The ribbon is divided into eight equal lengths. These lengths are then folded lengthwise diagonally and cut along this fold into two triangular pieces. Each piece is then gathered along its raw edge and arranged in a cascaded ruffle as shown in the illustration.

The wide ends of the sixteen lengths are each trimmed to a point, the other end being sewed down to a foundation

The Cascade Rosette

of fine net or buckram, thus forming the center. Flowers may be introduced, as illustrated. Made of narrower ribbon cut in shorter lengths a smaller rosette will result.

Butterfly Bow—(See Page 42)

Poinsettia Bow—(See Page 42)

Motifs for the Tailored Hat

Ornament No. 1

This ornament is developed from No. 12 Grosgrain Ribbon and requires 5/6 yards of material. Ribbon is folded as shown below completed ornament, making two clusters of three each, then join all together at center as shown and slash the ends. This makes a very effective bow, for finishing side crowns of tailored sailors.

Ornament No. 4

This plaited ribbon rosette is very simple to construct, and is formed of No. 9 Grosgrain by using 18-inch lengths laid in plaits as seen in larger view and fastened in the center, then fold same as in section below, and again fasten securely, and after forming 9 sections join all at center and finish by slashing ends.

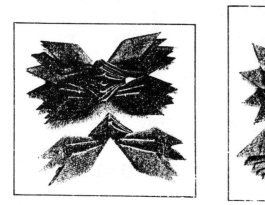

No. 1

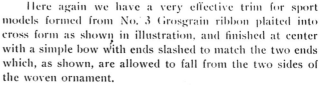

No. 2

No. 3

Ornament No. 2

Smart cockade effect with flying ends slashed. You will notice this also is formed of either No. 9 or No. 3 Grosgrain ribbon. If the No. 9 is used same should be folded through center, but in using the No. 3 this need not be done. Take a length of ribbon 11 inches and form a flat knot as seen in smaller picture, and secure with a concealed stitch and repeat this operation till you have formed 18 sections, then join all together at center.

Ornament No. 6

Here again we have a very effective trim for sport models formed from No. 3 Grosgrain ribbon plaited into cross form as shown in illustration, and finished at center with a simple bow with ends slashed to match the two ends which, as shown, are allowed to fall from the two sides of the woven ornament.

Ornament No. 3

This number is very good for trimming a small turban or roll brim style as it gives a very chic stick-up effect and may be developed from 2½ yards of No. 9 ribbon. This is formed as may be seen from section at the lower part of cut by making folded double section and fastened as seen, with ends folded back and ends slashed; form 16 of these sections, and finally join all together at center.

Ornament No. 7

Very smart bow effect, made from No. 3 Grosgrain ribbon, and requiring 2⅔ yards of material. This ornament is so very simple that it hardly requires any description, as one can readily see how same is formed, by making a series of side plaits and then all are joined at center, where they are secured by tying all together with the same width ribbon and slashing all ends.

Ornament No. 5

Here is an ornament in cabochon effect, formed by first making a small buckram cone the size desired, and then sew the different sections around, out from center, one plain strip, then a pleated strip with the three ends caught back, as can be easily seen in illustration. To finish center, fold a length of the ribbon through the center and roll up on center easily till you have enough to fill small opening.

No. 5

No. 4

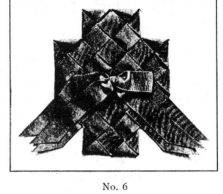

No. 7   No. 6   No. 8

Ornament No. 8

This ornament can be utilized in very many ways, and will naturally suggest itself to the trimmer. Again this is very simple to form, by using No. 3 Grosgrain ribbon, and make one length of plaiting, and then join to this five rows of the ribbon plain with a shirring string and draw up to form the fan effect, where a small tailored bow is used to finish at the center; then all the ends are slashed.

Smart and Unique Motifs for Hat Trimming

The Triple Bow is so named because everything about it is in groups of three.

There are three groups of loops, with three loops in each group, and three centers, as a finishing touch to this bow. It takes one and three-quarter yards of ribbon three inches wide to make the triple bow. The short loop is made of five and one-half inches, and the two loops under it, take respectively six inches, and six and one-half inches. The

Triple Bow

two under loops can be made in one continuous piece, the loops separated out, and stitched so they will stay that way, when the short loop is placed over them.

When the three groups are made, fasten them together at their base, merely stitching the edges together, leaving a hole in the center. Otherwise it cramps the center. Each loop must be made with little plaits at its base, all laid in the same direction and pulled into place, by putting the thumbs on the upper side of the ribbon, and the forefinger on the under side, with only one thickness of the silk between the thumbs and finger, and then give a gentle but firm stroke parallel to the selvage of the ribbon, and away from the plaits, and the ribbon will fall into beautiful folds, displaying the light and shadow of the silk to perfection.

The other end of the loop, must be plaited in the same manner, only the plait must lie in the opposite direction.

When these two ends are brought together to form the loop it will be found that the selvage of both sides will part equally. Whereas, if both ends were plaited alike, one side of the selvage would stand wide open, and the other would be tightly closed.

The center is composed of three separate strips, which go individually around each group. The end of one of these center pieces is plaited very fine, so as to take little space, and straight across the width of the ribbon. The other end is plaited in the same way, but slightly diagonal, so as to make the upper selvage shorter than the lower. Each time that a plait is made on the diagonal, it is reversed in direction from the first plaiting, and as you hold it firmly in the right hand, run your middle finger from underneath to the middle of the center, allowing only one thickness of the silk over the finger. This produces the fluted effect, in the middle of each center. The lower edge of the center, being longer than the upper edge, it extends downward, so that a needle may be drawn through the exact middle of the bow, and the three selvages, from the three drooping edges of the centers, can be caught with one stitch each, drawn together, and sewed fast on the wrong side one hole will be visible in the middle of the bow.

This bow is useful for the hat, and may be turned into a stickup, by doubling the length of the loops in one group. The triple bow looks well on the corsage and can be used in many delightful ways.

The Double Butterfly

The Double Butterfly Bow takes one and one-half yards of three-inch ribbon for its construction. The two standing pieces are cut separately. The lower one is sixteen inches long. Double it in the middle, across its width and measure off four inches from this center, along one of the selvages. Turn down the ends diagonally to the eight-inch selvage point and cut off the ends along this slope. If the line along which you cut is slightly curved outward, it will add to the artistic effect, although it be scarcely discernible to the eye.

Next plait the piece along the middle line, in very fine plaits and throw the thread around them, and cinch them up. Turn up the pointed ends so they face each other, and throw one more loop of the thread around the center, just above the plaiting to make a little stem.

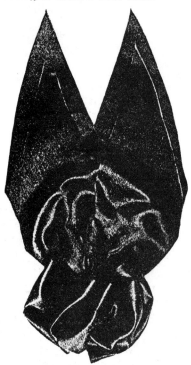

Double Butterfly Bow

The second standing piece is made exactly like the first, but its length is fourteen and one-half inches. This doubled in the middle, gives two pieces seven and one-quarter inches long. Mark off three and one-eighth inches, from the center, along one selvage, and cut to the point of the seven and one-quarter inch selvage. From this the process is identical with the first standing piece.

The second piece is now laid over the first one, and stitched down. A small tie stitch in each piece secures the ends and makes the proper parting of the points at the top.

A piece of ribbon twenty-two inches long is divided into five parts, each one being four and one-half inches in length. This is kept in one continuous piece. It is plaited and stroked as before described, at one end of the ribbon, and the plaiting reversed at the first four and one-half inches, and this alternating is repeated every four and one-half inches, until the whole piece is used. Turn it on the wrong side, bring the second plaiting up to the first end and stitch them together, making a loop. Form the next loop, and stitch it at its base to the second plaiting, the forth to the third and so on to the end.

This gives five loops, more or less elastic, so they can be arranged in a half moon about the base of the standing pieces, or they may be alternated, one inclining upward and the next downward, or they may be in a straight row. In any event, catch the middle loop first in its position, at the center of the base of the uprights, and then curve the ends, as desired, and stitch in place. If the loops were sewed solidly together, they would not give, but would stay in a solid lump.

The double butterfly, if used as a stickup, must be wired along the inner selvage of the standing pieces. This can be done before they are plaited, simply bringing the selvage over the wire on to the wrong side, and blind-stitching it down.

Aeroplane Bow

The Aeroplane Bow

The Aeroplane Bow requires fourteen inches of ribbon two and one-half inches wide. It is made in two pieces. The lower one is the longer. It is seven and one-half inches in length. Double it in the middle, measure off 2 inches from the center along one selvage, and slope the ends, as in the Double Butterfly. The smaller piece is 5 inches in length, double it across its width, mark off one and one-eighth inches along one selvage, from the double, and slope its ends in like manner to the first.

These two pieces are plaited very small, in their centers, and laid side by side with the short edges together.

Fasten them by a few stitches on the edge of the center of each piece, and take a separate piece of ribbon to cover this stitching, and complete the bow. This should be plaited at the top so that it would spread out, and then the plaiting should be reversed at the bottom, and drawn very tightly together so as to give this center of the bow a heart-like appearance.

Four of these bows, about the crown of a hat, and connected by a ribbon whose plaited ends are hidden under the bows, make a snappy trimming. The bows are placed

Water-lily Bow

equally distant from each other starting at the left front, and are so disposed on the side crown that the longer ends lie partly on the brim.

Water Lily Rosette

The Water Lily Rosette is made of one and one-half or two-inch ribbon. There are sixteen pieces, each five and one-half inches long, which are fish-tailed, as in the sunflower rosette. Take each of these pieces, and lay them in two plaits, lengthwise, each plait taking half the width of the ribbon. Let the plaits be in the same direction, and press them in place with a moderate iron. Take two pieces, lay them across each other, at right angles, and stitch firmly together, in the center. Two more pieces, at right angles, are placed over the first ones, so as to space this beginning of the rosette, into eight parts. Then the rosette is built up, always with two pieces at right angles, so spaced as to fill all the interstices of the ends. The last four pieces are caught with the thread over their center, and cinched down firmly in the middle of the rosette. Too much stress cannot be laid upon the necessity of using very strong thread and pulling it very tight in this construction.

After the rosette is sewed, go over each petal with the fingers, pulling it sharply upward and arranging the general appearance artistically, when it will be found to closely resemble the water lily, from which it gets its name.

This is a very pretty rosette for children's hats, or for the hair. It can be made in different shades of the same color, or in contrasting colors. It is useful to the milliner to use up short ends of ribbon.

The Tailored Ladder Bow

The Tailored Ladder Bow is made of ribbon the same width as that of the sunflower rosette. Each bow requires five and one-quarter inches of ribbon. Turn in one-quarter of an inch at each end, as shown in the piece of constructive ribbon "A," turn under the lower corner, and bring down this end, along the lower selvage, as also shown in "A." Now double the bow lengthwise, and the flap that comes over to the lower selvage, must be fastened by inserting the needle from the back about the center of the side of the flap, and let the needle pass along in the diagonal fold of the side of the flap, until it is very near the bottom, where it should pierce the ribbon on to the wrong side, where it can be secured. Both ends of the bow being finished in

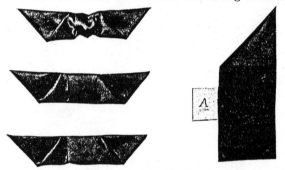

The Tailored Ladder Bow

this way, the center is put on perfectly flat, and should be of the same width of the bow. These bows may be used in groups of three and connected by a ribbon, folded to the exact width as the bow center.

Hence their name—Ladder Bows.

A totally different effect can be given by making two little plaits under the bow center, both laid in the same direction. The center, also, has one plait at each end reversed from each other, which raises the middle slightly.

These bows may be used singly, in pairs, or threes; the connecting piece may be omitted and they can be made of silk, velvet, leather, or any fabric that is not transparent. They are unique for the corsage of a dress, or singly, can be worn at the neck.

The Fancy Alsatian Bow

The Fancy Alsatian Bow is made of two pieces of three-inch ribbon, each of which is eight and one-half inches long. The ends are all fishtailed, and both pieces plaited, in the middle of their length. They are then laid across each other, so the ends will be slightly apart. Sew the two pieces together, where they cross each other. Take fifteen inches of the ribbon and lay it off in five sections of three

inches each. Plait it exactly as in the Double Butterfly Bow, but do not bend it into a crescent. Place the loops in the center of the two crossed pieces, and sew down the middle loop first, then the end ones. The central loop can be curved like the letter "S," and its ends stitched down, so that it will retain its shape. This bow, when made larger, is beautiful for hat trimming, or made of narrower ribbon or velvet is fine for the neck.

The Sunflower Rosette

The Sunflower Rosette takes three yards of ribbon, anywhere from one and one-half to two inches wide. If you ask for ribbon one and one-half inches wide, you will be told there is no ribbon made of that width, and if you ask for two-inch ribbon, it will not measure that wide. So take your choice, but any of these widths will make the rosette. Cut sixteen pieces, each six inches long. This

Fancy Alsatian Bow

requires two and two-thirds yards of the ribbon. Each of these pieces must be fishtailed at either end. This is done by folding the ribbon in the middle, lengthwise, so the two selvages come together, then at the end, bend the center of the ribbon out to the selvage, so that the upper edge of the end will lie parallel and just over the selvage. Cut across the diagonal double and it gives the notched effect called fishtailing. Next fold the ribbon in the middle from top to bottom, and then fold again across its center, from side to side. Bend the notched ends upward together and then part them out, until one overlaps the other, for about one-third of its width. This is shown in the first fold of ribbon, at the side of the rosette. Take one small plait at the bottom, as shown in the second fold of ribbon, and stitch it in place. All sixteen pieces are similarly treated, observing carefully all the while, that all the points of the rosette are in the same direction, that the overlapping end always comes from the same side, and that the plait at the bottom, is of the same depth, and in the same direction, with each part.

The sixteen pieces are then laid together, overlapping each other at the bottom by half their width. When the lower part is sewed into a ring, the upper part is tie stitched into position, about half way from the center to the outer or notched edge. The tie stitch is made through the lower side of each notched piece, and merely pierces one thickness below it. So no stitches are visible from the outside.

For Milady's Boudoir

Ribbons are essentially feminine and a woman's career might almost be written in them.
Charming Gift Articles Useful Throughout the Year.

Some Fascinating Ribbon-made Articles to Brighten up the Ribbon Counter

The illustration features a charming negligee and boudoir cap. One of the new telephone screens in the shape of a dainty
Rococo lady; a lampshade of novel design; candle shades, and all the fascinating dainties intended for milady's
comfort and the embellishment of her dressing table

One Hundred and One Hand-made Novelties for all Occasions
YOU CAN MAKE THEM   YOU CAN SELL THEM
Particularly Suitable for Gifts

There is no ribbon scrap, no bit of silk or velvet so inconsequential that it cannot be put to excellent use, making charming Xmas gifts, which sell on sight, and at very fair prices. A very successful milliner who owns two stores, saves the smallest pieces of silk, velvet and plush, besides bits of braid, buckram and wire, and each year this accumulation with stray flowers, feathers and ornaments is made into doll hats, of various sizes and styles. These find ready sale for the Christmas holidays and are exhibited in the windows on doll models, many of which are dressed to match the hats, and sold entire. They make an attraction when on display that no child can resist.

Novelties Made of Scraps

A few suggestions of utilizing scraps that may be found in any milliner's workroom are given herewith. Take the cute little Japanese dollies (they may be bought for a very few cents at any department store) which lend themselves readily to the making of pen wipers, and needle cases. Of a scrap of gaily colored silk or tinseled goods make a kimono for each doll. The arms are extended by a wooden tooth pick, stitched into the sleeves, and the needle case is held apparently by the hands, falling from them in triangular folds. Each fold is buttonholed in color, and small bows are used at the hands. The pen wiper is an apron extending to the bottom of the skirt in several folds and ornamented with a bow right in front at the waist line.

A satin-covered tambourin, a handy article for the dressing table is made of two cardboard disks measuring about 3 inches in diameter, and held together by means of tiny overcast stitches. The top is decorated with a flower motif made of ribbon, and the side is encompassed by narrower ribbon. Three ribbon loops descend from the base of the tambourin. The two longer ones hold a bone ring which serves for holding safety pins, while from the shorter loop a tiny doll in the shape of a pincushion is suspended.

Lingerie Ribbon Container

A pretty container for the indispensable bolt of baby ribbon is shown at the right side of the cut. To make this as illustrated procure a medium large doll's head with curly hair, fastening it to a little satin bag, slashed in the center front to hold the ribbon roll. The end of the ribbon is drawn through the doll's mouth, and will always be found to run freely, and never become entangled. Four strips of

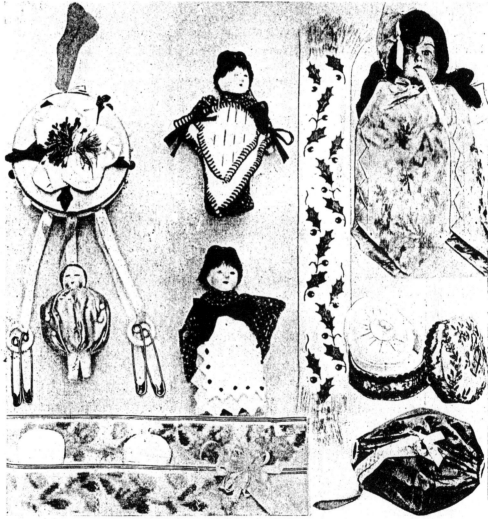

wide fancy ribbon afford the doll's dress. They are joined along the selvages by means of cat-stitching and mitred at the lower ends. A little hood of the same ribbon and trimmed with little bows completes the attractive novelty.

Another very popular receptacle for the ribbon bolt is shown on the lower right-hand corner of the illustration. It is made of a half yard of fancy taffeta ribbon, shirred along each edge and fastened to a ribbon-covered brass or bone ring. The ends are seamed but not joined and through them the bolt of ribbon is inserted. The bag will hold two bolts,

Corsage bouquets, featuring the new vanity flowers with powder-box centers. The ribbon loops contain small mirrors.

concealed all the little trifles so necessary to Madame's or Mademoiselle's comfort: powder box, powder puff and mirror. Our illustrations show a rose, a tiger lily, a chrysanthemum, a spray of orchids, a clematis with buds and a dahlia.

The rose, a full-blown American Beauty, consists of ten petals, made of four-inch satin ribbon, each petal made double, mitred near the top, and crushed so as to produce a most realistic effect. The inner petals are grouped about a little box containing French face powder in solid form. The little lamb's wool puff contained in each box is finished at the top with a little shirred puffing of ribbon in the tone of the rose, or else with a millinery flower in a tone harmonizing with that of the rose, and selected in the exact size of the puff or a trifle larger to hold the puff firmly in the box, preventing it from falling out. A tiny ribbon-wound ring is fastened to the center of the puff covering. Sprays of natural foliage accompany the rose. For the tiger lily, as well as the clematis and the orchid, it will be best to procure the flowers already made, fastening the little powder box in the center of each flower, and treating the puff in the manner described with reference to the rose described above. The foliage is replaced by loops of leaf green satin ribbon—one, two or three, as desired. The longest of these loops, which measures about six inches, is sewed into a little pocket, in which a small mirror is inserted. The mirror should be procured before the ribbon is selected for the loops.

The Vanity chrysanthemum, one of the most attractive effects, is very easily made, requiring a bolt of narrow ribbon (a size wider than baby ribbon), in a pretty shade of yellow, pink or mauve, unless white is preferred. The ribbon is at regular intervals tied into loose knots, forming very realistic looking chrysanthemum petals, which are grouped about the powder box, after this has been covered

the ends of each to be passed through one of the rings. The holder is suspended from a ribbon loop with bow.

For the lingerie ribbon container at the left take 14 inches of ribbon, 5 inches wide. Fold over one-third of its width and divide it into four parts, feather stitching as illustrated. This forms three pockets to hold pasteboard cards of lingerie tape. The end is finished by folding in the corners of the ribbon, and putting a very narrow ribbon rosette on its peak, and facing on the opposite side from the pockets.

The most prosaic-looking powder box may be made decidedly elaborate by covering it with a bit of brocade or other fancy fabric, finishing it with rows of silk or metal gimp. No directions are necessary, but care must be taken to apply the fabric smoothly and neatly, and to use colorless glue that will not stain.

Ribbons in varying widths can be profitably made into bookmarks. Overcast two lengths together, on both selvages, fringe the ends, and slip in a piece of buckram, or paper, simply to make it stiff enough, so it will not have to be unfolded all the time. One of these adds greatly to the attractiveness of a gift book, or is a sweet little remembrance, in itself. One made of holly ribbon with fringed ends is here shown.

Vanity Flowers

For several seasons the corsage bouquet has been relied upon for brightening up Winter costumes and wraps of heavy fabrics or fur, and they have filled their purpose so extremely well that they have found a permanent place in Milady's Midwinter outfit. The latest and most perfect evolution in artificial bouquets is the Vanity flower, a cleverly conceived novelty suitable for the decoration of the tailor-made suit as well as the afternoon gown or evening toilette. It is not only highly ornamental in itself, but does away with the nuisance of having to carry a bag, for in it are

with a width of the ribbon, shirred and tightly drawn in at the base, to fit the box snugly. This covering greatly facilitates the joining of the petals firmly to the powder box.

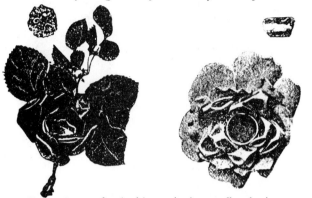

Vanity flowers fitted with powder-box, puff and mirror

A handsome collar and cuff set made of Roman ribbon

The center is of brown chenille and equipped with a little ring. The flower is completed by a spray of natural foliage, and is accompanied by two ribbon loops, one four, the other seven inches long. The latter contains the little mirror.

The dahlia is made by doubling 4-inch ribbon and folding it along the two selvages, forming irregular pleats, which are tacked to place about a ribbon-covered powder box, and is finished with a spray of foliage and ornamented with a long and a short ribbon loop and an end cut off diagonally. The

Miniature band-box for vanity flowers

Boxes may be covered with chintz, cretonne, figured silk or fancy paper

longer loop is made into a pocket for the mirror. The powder box, puff and the arrangement of the petals are shown in detail in the illustration.

Girdle and wreath for a young girl's evening gown. Everything but the foliage is made of ribbon.

Fancy reticule of brocade, girdle and neckruff of striped ribbon

Gifts Pleasing and Profitable Made of Short Lengths of Ribbon

Corset Bag. Workbag of Dresden ribbon and crochet rings. Corsage ornaments. Ladies' Tailored Tie.

Brush and Buttonhook Holder. Safety Pin Holder. Face Powder Puff and Cleaner. Lingerie Ribbon Holder. Boat-shaped Pin Cushion. Fancy Garter with Jewel Case attached. Individual Skirt Hangers. Four-in-hand Tie

Ribbon sashes are as popular as they ever were, and are especially well liked by the younger set. Our illustration shows an unusually attractive one of soft, brocaded fancy ribbon. It consists of a long loop and two rounded ends, and is adorned with an oblong buckle, with hooks and eyes or patent buttons. The same illustration features a decorative hair band for the young girl. To make it, a wire ring sufficiently large in diameter to fit the wearer's head comfortably is covered with ruched fancy ribbon. The large double bow may be worn, as desired at the front, side or back of the head, according to the arrangement of the coiffure. Elastic may be substituted for the wire, in which case the band will make a suitable decoration for a boudoir cap.

Wide, supple satin ribbon furnished the material for the

dainty boudoir cap shown herewith. It has a circular center part measuring 6 inches in diameter, to which 1½ yards of sash ribbon is shirred. After shirring the lower part, the ribbon is arranged in flat folds, and each fold held in place by a tiny flower made of gauze ribbon with a bright yellow French knot or a gold bead in the center. A frill of fine lace is set under the cap, forming a graceful edge finish and at the same time constituting the lining. A little crescent motif of the flowers set over the center front and two irregularly long ends of the ribbon which descend from the center back complete the dainty cap.

Baby's Clothes Hanger
of Satin Ribbon

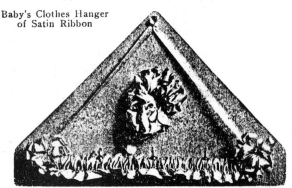

Baby rack, made of 1¼ yard 3-inch ribbon shirred on ⅝ yard of 1½-inch ribbon with bows at extreme ends of strip, left for hanger. A soft round stick slipped on makes a solid foundation for screws or hooks.

The armlets are made of ¾-inch satin, doubled and gathered on both edges, and fulled over elastic. Rosettes of baby ribbon add a pleasing finish.

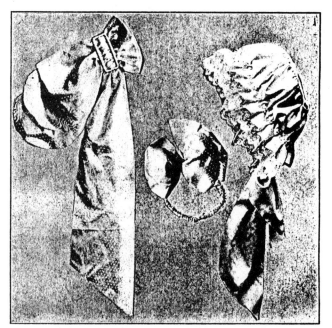

Girdle, coiffure band and breakfast cap of ribbon

*Straw-
berry
Cluster
Sachet
and
Pin
Cushion*

The most inconsequential bits
of ribbon are utilized for these
fascinating little sachets, which
also serve as pin cushions, and
the cost is only the two yards of
baby ribbon and sachet powder.
Selling for 35 cents a cluster
gives a good profit to the milliner.

Folding Work Basket

Made of flowered silk with plain
silk lining. The interior of the
bag is fitted with scissors, bodkin,
needle case and other sewing
utensils held in place by means
of stitched straps.

Hat Pin Holder

This vase hat pin holder
proved one of the best sellers
in a millinery store.   Thirty
inches of No. 16 ribbon makes
the rose top and one bolt of
baby ribbon is required for the
rosettes.   The vase cost five
cents and the holder complete
sells for $1.00.

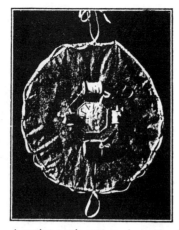

A pocket work case can be made of
small scraps of ribbon and is a convenient little article to own.   It will
carry four spools of thread, a package
of needles and a thimble at the least,
and may be made to accommodate
tape, braid and a small pair of scissors.

Giant Strawberry

When the familiar strawberry
shape cushion is made in good
size, of beautiful scarlet satin
ribbon with calyx of green, the
sale is almost unlimited. Sixteen
inches of 8-inch scarlet ribbon
is required with one yard of
half-inch green satin ribbon for
the calyx.

Oblong Pincushion

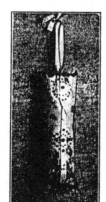

Pretty though simple cushion of brocade ribbon.

Pincushion of
Dresden Ribbon

This pincushion
is made of four
strips of figured
ribbon stitched to-
gether and fastened
at the top with a
bow of narrow rib-
bon. A square of
cardboard covered
with ribbon forms
the bottom of this
little square silk
sack, which is
stuffed with cot-
ton perfumed with
sachet powder. Pins
of various sizes and
colors are thrust in
the figured portions,
and larger pins are
placed along the
seams.

Folding Case for Ribbons, etc.

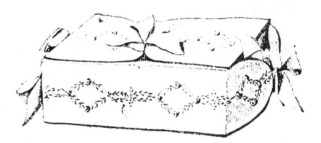

This traveling case, meant to hold ribbons, veils, etc., is simply
held together by bows of ribbon, and when these are united it can
be laid perfectly flat in one's suit case or trunk with the veils, etc.,
folded on the top of it, ready to be tied up when the case is lifted
out. The cardboard foundation is covered on one side only, with
a pretty brocaded ribbon for the outside, and plain for the inside.

Dainties for the
Dressing Table

The circular pin-
cushion is made of a
wire strainer with a
silk covered founda-
tion, and edged with
a frill of ribbon. Can
be made easily at 20
cents, sells at 50 cents.
The leg-shaped pin-
cushion makes a pretty
gift for one's men
friends, and is as sim-
ple to make as it is
attractive. It sells at
from 50 to 75 cents,
but can be made at
less than half.   The
small   pendant bells
are very christmasy
and pleasing and sell
readily.   The card-
board forms are cov-
ered with holly ribbon
and suspended from
strips of baby ribbon.
They may be scented
with sachet.   The
cluster retails at about
35 cents.

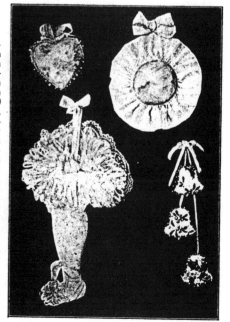

Fancy Articles of Ribbon
FOR HOLIDAY GIFTS AND DECORATIVE PURPOSES

A pretty coat hanger is made by winding a wire hanger with ribbon and tying a bow at each end. Two scented hearts are suspended by baby ribbon from the hanger at the center.

Lavender ribbon is used for the example shown, and the entire hanger is wound with a very narrow number. Baby ribbon may be used. Two hearts in a lavender color, with tiny four-looped bows and suspending ribbons serve to decorate the hanger and provide a delicate scent.

At either end of the hanger a bow is placed consisting of three loops, and one end and two loops and two ends respectively. No 60 ribbon is used in a taffeta or satin ribbon. The loops are 3 inches deep and the ends 4 inches long. The bows consume 1½ yards of ribbon and 5 yards of baby ribbon should be allowed.

A Little Sewing Apron

A little sewing bag which serves as an apron for protecting the lap is made of two strips of wide printed ribbon sewed together lengthwise. The ends are shirred over embroidery rings which are wound with ribbon one inch wide and decorated with bows and ends of the same ribbon.

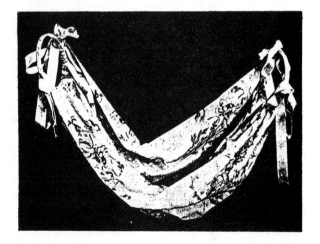

This little, simply constructed article is a combination of apron and work bag. When not in use it is hung up

by the rings and holds the work being done, together with scissors, thread, needles, pins, etc. Where one must work in midst of interruptions this is a very convenient arrangement, since the work can be caught up and disposed of easily.

One and a quarter yards of wide, printed ribbon and five yards of narrow ribbon harmonizing with it, are needed, with two small embroidery rings. The wide ribbon is cut in two equal lengths and sewed in an overlaid seam together to increase the width of the ribbon.

Decorative Bag

A decorative handkerchief bag designed for the toilet table or dressing case is pictured in this illustration. One

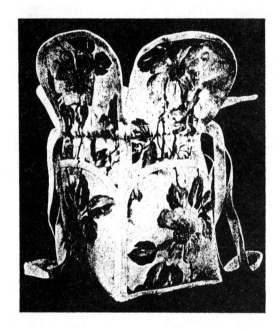

should select, to make it, a wide, boldly flowered brocaded or printed ribbon. If intended for a present the ribbon may be selected with reference to the season or other circumstance. For Christmas, the poinsettia flower or holly, for Easter the lily, etc. Ribbon not narrower than No. 100 will be required; flowered silk may be used also. Four yards of No. 100 ribbon will make the bag or case.

The bottom is made of cardboard cut in a square the sides of which are ¼ inch shorter than the width of the ribbon. It is covered with a layer or two of cotton batting on one side over which a plentiful amount of sachet powder is sprinkled. This cotton is basted to the square of cardboard and it is then covered with thin silk or other material of a light weave through which the odor of the powder will penetrate. Four similar covered pieces are made except that one side of each square is rounded instead of straight.

Acceptable Gifts for Baby and Mother

Pretty Trifles of Practical Use

The little doll has a flannel petticoat, meant to hold safety pins, and a dress of fancy ribbon. Fancy hand-painted ribbon was used for making the coat hanger and the little sachet, while the novelty rattle shows an embroidery hoop wound and spanned with narrow ribbon and finished with tiny bells. A set of these little articles sells as high as $3.00, but can be made for very much less.

Dainty Gifts for the Baby

The padded coat hangers, the little trinket box, the safety pin holder and circular pin cushion are all intended for baby's trousseau, and are as easily copied as they are attractive.

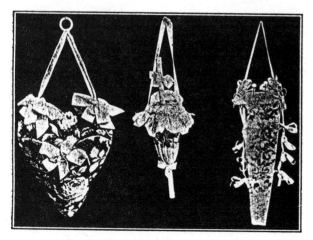

For Whisk Broom, Pins and Hat Pins

The whisk broom holder is made of two heart-shaped pieces of cardboard (one two inches higher than the other), covered with flowered silk and suspended from a ribbon loop. It will easily bring 50 cents, though it can be made for about 20 cents.

The pincushion simulates a parasol and is made of flowered fancy ribbon and stuffed with chaff or sawdust. Frills of lace finish the top. The hat pin holder is shaped like an inverted obelisk, and its cardboard foundation is masked with fancy ribbon. A little frill of lace finishes the edge and tiny ribbon bows complete the pretty article.

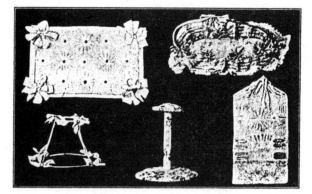

Useful Novelties Easily Made

This illustration shows a case for baby's bonnet ties, an oval pin cushion, two bonnet rests and a cord for holding various fancy and safety pins. These articles are so easily copied as not to require any special directions, and they will make Xmas gifts that sell on sight and at a very fair profit.

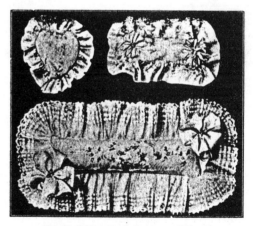

Pin Cushions Both Large and Small

There is a constant demand for pincushions, which are as popular as gifts for children as for grown-ups. The small models retail at 50 and 35 cents respectively, while the large oblong cushion will easily bring $1.50.

Fancy Ribbon Garments

The printed and fancy ribbons make up into exquisite matinees, small kimonos and all the dainty house garments which the home-keeping woman is privileged to use. Their flowered patterns and rich colorings render them very effective for all the bretelles, jumpers, coats, etc., cut on Oriental lines, which have attained a vogue that promises to remain for some time. They are especially effective in the dainty Louis XV coats, where with the addition of rhinestone buttons and pretty laces they appear at their best. Their intricate patterns allow of much shaping and piecing, and just the same effects are not to be evolved from any other material.

Fancy Hand Bags of Ribbon Always in Vogue

(Shown on opposite page)

Fancy bags are among the most popular and most acceptable gifts for all occasions. We are here showing a number of the most attractive ones, all possessing the chief advantage of being easily and inexpensively copied. There is, for instance, the commodious reticule, that has recently been reintroduced and welcomed with great enthusiasm. The one shown in No. 1 is made of heavy satin, but it can also be made of wide ribbon, four strips about 15 inches long, which are sewed together, mitred along the ends and finished with a long tassel. The bag thus formed is lined and shirred along the top, after which it is joined to a gate lock, to which ribbon loops are fastened. A smaller bag of figured brocade is also shown.

A charming evening bag (No. 2) is made of ¾ of a yard of sash ribbon, doubled, sewed together to within 5 inches from the top, and lined with soft silk in a contrasting tone. The top is finished with slashes and is separated from the bag proper by means of a double row of machine stitching. Inch-wide ribbon is inserted. The dainty bag

the center of the larger bag, and is intended as a receptacle for the powder puff, while the larger compartment may be used for purse, opera glasses and handkerchief.

A very useful little bag is that shown in the opposite corner. It is made of flowered silk in pastel tints, cut 12 inches wide and about 25 inches long, and it is sewed to an oval of cardboard covered with the figured silk and lined with the same plain silk with which the bag is lined. Ribbon draw strings complete the bag.

The largest of the fancy bags is conspicuous by great elegance, being made of gold and passementerie gimp in a handsome lace design, and lined with old rose moiré, covered with gold tulle. The front is 6 inches shorter than the back, and the top is shirred to a hoop covered with silk and gold gimp. (An ordinary embroidery hoop will do for this purpose). A pendant motif of silk passementerie completes the bag, which is embellished with tiny chiffon flowers in pink and pastel blue, scattered at random over the entire surface of the bag.

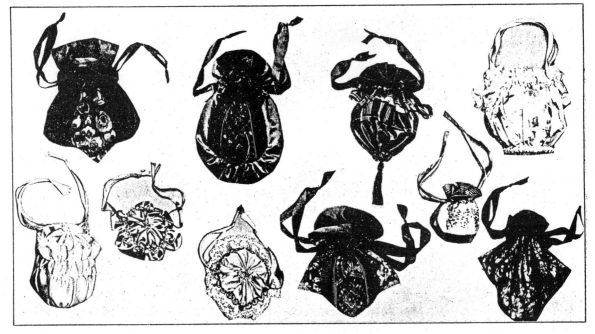

Bags for the Opera Glasses, the Fancy Work and the Vanity Box

is decorated with a hand-made rose, made of bias folds of chiffon, and finished with a leaf of the same fabric.

Of the ten bags pictured, five are very elaborate, while the remaining five were designed with a view to serviceability. The most interesting among these latter is the "overnight bag" (No. 3) made of soft satin and lined with light Japanese silk. It requires 1½ yards of each kind of silk, 3 inches wide, which is stitched together along the top. At the base the lined bag is folded in, envelope style, and the flap thus formed gathered in with the top. Thus a pocket is formed, which serves as a receptacle for comb, brushes, nail file and other toilet articles required for overnight stops. The large pocket formed by the bag itself contains the night-dress, kimono, boudoir cap and slippers.

The graceful vanity bag shown in illustration (No. 4) is made of a circular piece of figured silk, measuring 15 inches in diameter. This is finished with a plain silk lining, and within 2 inches from the edge, is equipped with a casing with ribbon draw strings. A smaller bag, made and lined exactly like the one just described, is sewed to

In the upper left corner is shown a graceful little theater bag of dull blue taffeta to which a large beaded motif in delicate coloring has been applied. The top is finished with a frill of pleated lace, while a beaded fringe finishes the base.

Opposite this is shown a dressy little handbag meant to complete the afternoon gown. It is made of two ovals of satin, 5 inches wide and 9 inches long, stitched together and covered with gold tulle to which gold bands were applied. These are studded with tiny rosebuds of chiffon. The opening of the bag is oval and placed near the top of the front, and the closing flap is equipped with a little oval mirror, and held in place with a patent button. Silk cord and a long silk tassel add a harmonious finishing touch.

The small bag (No. 10) is made of a strip of turquoise blue taffeta, daintily trimmed with frills of lace and graceful appliqué garlands of ribbon rosebuds. The top is finished with ruched Valenciennes lace, while the lower edge is shirred to the gold gimp outlining a little circular mirror.

BAGS FOR ALL PURPOSES EASILY AND CHEAPLY MADE

(See Page 58 for description)

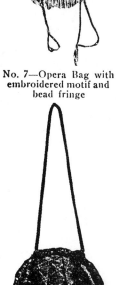

No. 7—Opera Bag with
**embroidered motif and
bead fringe**

No. 8—Theatre Bag fitted
with mirror

There never
was a gift
more welcome
to young and
old than a bag,
and, as fashion
favors them,
there is an un-
limited variety
including bags
for the house
and bags for
the street, the
dressing table
and the work
basket. Rib-
bon, wide and
narrow, piece
silk and velvet,
brocade and
lace, all are
suitable for be-
ing made into
bags.

All of these
designs may
easily be re-
produced, us-
ing left-over
stock or short
ends for both
making and
decorating
them. Various
ornamental
motifs, such as
are found in
every milliner's
workroom may
be used to
great advan-
tage for finish-
ing the more
elaborate styles
here shown.

No. 2—A dainty Evening Bag
for the débutante

No. 1—One of the popular commodious
Reticules

No. 6—A large elaborate bag
for dress occasions

No. 9
Reticule with embroidery
and passementerie appliqué

The Over-
night bag is
exceedingly
practical, con-
sisting of a
large and a
smaller com-
partment. The
latter contains
toilet requisites
needed for an
overnight stop.

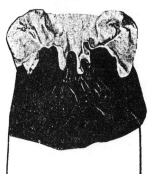

No. 3
Overnight Bag in
black and white

No. 10—Bag for the
powder puff

No. 5—Workbag of
flowered silk

No. 4—Fancy double bag

Hand-Craft Bags
MAKE IDEAL GIFTS FOR ALL OCCASIONS

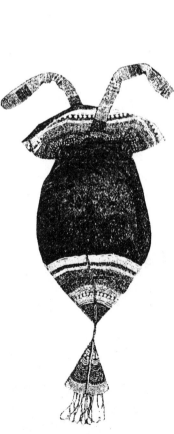

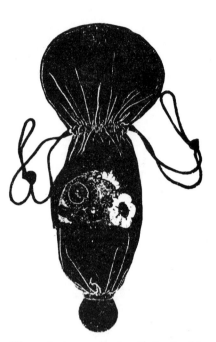

A dainty bag suitable for theater use. The upper part is of soft taffeta coming out of a calyx-like base of velvet in a contrasting tone. Fruits made of velvet and hand-embroidery garnish each alternate velvet scallop.

A serviceable bag with black velvet top and lower part of light-colored taffeta stitched to form squares. Bouquets of ribbon flowers and a drooping cluster of ball motifs in contrasting tints afford the decoration.

The ancient *aumonière* bag is simulated in this charming model, which in the original was developed of dull blue velvet, with three-toned velvet piping, and beaver pompon finish. The garniture accentuates the mediaeval effect produced by the bag, showing a large appliqué motif formed by felt and velvet flowers, hand embroidered and beaded, and showing brilliant coloring.

An old-fashioned but strikingly new beaded bag. The background is of dark iridescent beads, while the design is carried out in vividly colored Venetian beads. The bag is drawn together by means of silk cords drawn through crochet rings fastened to the outside top.

An uncommonly attractive bag of soft satin, top and tapering lower part of solid beads in Egyptian coloring. The handles, too, are of beads, and so is the conical and fringe-finished ornament finishing the base.

A new version of the Marguerite bag, made of heavy faille silk, the lower part entirely of beads in a lattice pattern carried out in two colors. Further ornamentation is introduced by triangular lattice motifs done in heavy silk thread, and small passementerie grelots of silk and gold. The handles, to correspond with the lower part of the bag, are of beads.

Dainty Trinkets
SERVICEABLE ALL   THE YEAR

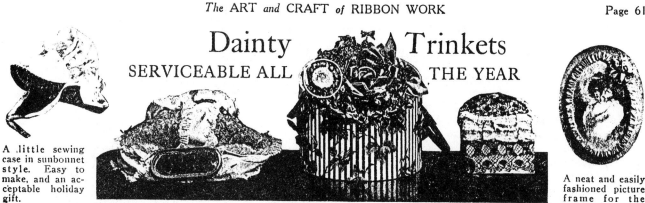

A little sewing case in sunbonnet style. Easy to make, and an acceptable holiday gift.

Fancy bag with mirror base

Vanity bouquet and box (the ring indicates powder puff)

Jewel case with cushion top

A neat and easily fashioned picture frame for the boudoir.

A handy and ornamental catch-all bag is made of one yard of 5½-inch ribbon, by laying the ribbon double the height of its width, sewing the selvages together at the back (the depth of the triangular fold) to form a pocket and fastening both overlapping ends under the overlap. The heart-shape is produced by drawing in the outer selvage of the overlapping pieces where they join the overlap. The bag is all in one piece and is trimmed with tiny bows of baby ribbon, and finished with a loop to hang it up.

Work Cases

The attractive work cases here featured are, as elegant as they seem, very easily copied. One of particularly attractive design of which an illustration appears on page 55, is shaped like an inverted hat. To make this, cut two circles, one of figured, the other of plain silk (each about 15 inches in diameter), stitch them together after a cardboard or other stiffening has been inserted at the center, and complete the case by adding to it a stitched handle of the material. Stitched straps are sewed to the lining and serve for holding scissors, needle case, emory bag and other sewing needfuls. The other case shows the shape of a satchel and is covered with black and white striped silk, and lined in bright red satin. A small circular bag secured by a drawstring

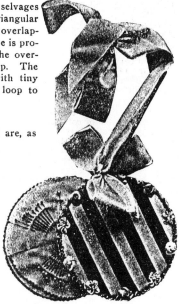

Circular needle case of striped ribbon. The cardboard disks measure 8 inches in diameter and are covered as illustrated.

is fastened to the central one of the three sections forming the case, while to the upper and lower section are fastened a needlebook and straps holding emory bag, bodkin, scissors and a small darner. Shirred handles of ribbon complete the case.

The square jewel box on the other side of the bandbox is not at all intricate to make, and very small scraps may be utilized in copying it. Any little square box may be used; cover it with faille or taffeta silk in any desired shade, stretching gold or silver lace over the silk. The lid is equipped with hinges and its top firmly padded, to form a pincushion, after which it is first covered with the silk and then with metal lace and finished with several rows of shirred or pleated Valenciennes lace. The interior of the box as well as the lid is lined in a contrasting tone and finished with narrow gold or silver gimp.

It is essential that in all cases where delicate fabrics in pale tints have to be kept in place by pasting, the glue employed must be colorless so as not to be visible and not to spot the material. There are several excellent millinery glues in the market which, beside having the best of adhesive qualities may be used with perfect safety on the frailest tissues and the most delicate colorings.

Heart-shaped catch-all bag of flowered ribbon

Lamb's wool slipper sole, for powdering back, neck and arms. Can be made at a cost of 30 cents, will sell at 75 cts.

Fitted work case in black and white ribbon, lined with scarlet satin. Two views.

Hand-Craft Motifs
Profitable Workroom Products

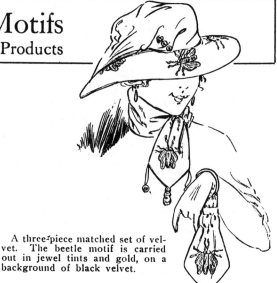

A three-piece matched set of velvet. The beetle motif is carried out in jewel tints and gold, on a background of black velvet.

Given a box of beads, a few skeins of embroidery silk, metal thread, worsteds and chenille there is simply no limit to the milliner's possibilities in devising highly artistic and decorative trimming motifs. Her scrap box will be a wonderful help, for it contains veritable treasures. Every tiniest bit of silk, of velvet or ribbon, every scrap of lace, gimp or tinseled tissue can thus be put to excellent use, and while practically of no intrinsic value, these left-over remnants may be turned into merchandise that not only sells on sight, but, being so much in demand at present, sells at extremely good prices.

Fashion favors garnitures hand-made: hand-embroidered, hand-beaded, hand-crocheted, and the milliner who is alert will avail herself of the suggestion here given. She will prepare hand-made ornaments before the season is at its height, when neither she nor her helpers have the necessary time to devote to the making of them. When forced to buy them, she will soon discover that she could have made a great many of these trimming motifs for the price asked for one of the imported novelties.

There are so many different forms of trimming motifs that can be made more attractive by the addition of a little

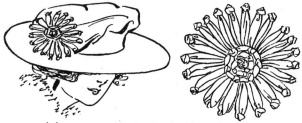

A huge marguerite made of white satin ribbon deftly knotted

handwork. Fur trimmings, for instance. In a stunning imported hat, a wide-brimmed sailor of deep blue velvet, the trimming consists of a large star of moleskin, appliquéd to the front of the crown. This is held in place by silver thread in long-and-short stitch. It goes without saying that the brim edge is finished with a fur band to match the trimming motif, likewise outlined with these silver stitches. Without a doubt the hat, though really very simple, will bring from $30 to $35 when sold by the importer. It may

A graceful Watteau basket of chenille and silver braid, filled with hand-made flowers

be produced in very excellent material for about one-fifth of that sum.

The detail sketches shown herewith feature some of the latest forms of hand-made millinery motifs, in embroidery, bead work, appliqué, etc. Besides these there are countless other methods in which the milliner can demon-

strate her ingenuity, reducing at the same time the store of scraps which accumulate in every workroom. From bits of velvet, taffeta or satin very attractive flowers can be

A simple but highly decorative pattern in "lazy daisy" stitch, done in chenille and gold embroidery on satin

made by cutting petals out of the material, and joining them to form flowers. (To make these more realistic, pad them with cotton and supplement them with stems, calyxes and foliage.

Conventionalized butterfly in Oriental colors. The wire foundation is wound with chenille and filled in with a lattice of beads. Antennae of chenille-wound wire

Large-petaled, flat flowers are those best suited for reproduction in ribbon or piece goods. The poppy is a popular style, very easily reproduced; so are the anemone, the clematis, the wild rose, the poinsettia and the jessamine. Fruits, such as peaches, apples, plums and pears, also grapes, are sometimes combined with these hand-made flowers, and are very decorative, indeed, when padded and applied in *bas-relief* effect, to either the crown or brim of a hat.

Moss roses of ribbon; stems and foliage of green chenille on thin wire forms

A much-liked style is to embroider large ornamental figures in bright wool or heavy silk on a ground of large-

Brim edge of Vandyck points done in wool. Embroidered cherries in natural color worked on crown direct.
Detail sketch shows soutache embroidery filled in with worsted

meshed Brussels net, which is then draped over the crown of a hat or toque. These patterns are very easily copied in long-and-short or Kensington stitch, and wonderful trimming effects à la Bakst may thus be produced at a mere

A dainty motif in chenille embroidery in delicate tints. Can also be made of heavy yarn. Splendid for sports hats

fraction of the price one has to pay for these novelties. The same applies to the rich Bulgarian and Russian embroidery bands done in cross-stitch and generally outlined with bands of fur. A yard-long strip of these imported bandings

A crown wreath embroidered in satin stitch with fine wool in old-fashioned tones

ranges from three to five dollars; it can be produced for almost nothing if the milliner applies a strip of embroidery scrim to an equally wide strip of broadcloth or heavy silk, and works a cross-stitch border of any desired pattern (even

Bulgarian band done in red, blue and yellow cross-stitch on a foundation of broadcloth edged with fur

a child can copy a cross-stitch pattern from an embroidery book), after which the scrim is drawn away thread by thread, and the embroidery, thus transferred on the broadcloth or silk, remains.

Ribbon is used for making the most fascinating of

An antique Roman design, worked in chenille and beads (in Paisley colors) on a stiffened foundation. A popular motif for crown trimming

Floral spray, with hand-made flowers of silk and velvet leaves applied to hat in large buttonhole stitch of yarn

garnitures, and here, too, the treasure trove of the scrap box may be exploited. One clever milliner designed a lovely trimming for a small, high toque of Bordeaux duvetyne,

Flat appliqué motif, traced in tiny silver beads and filled in with long stitches of worsted in bright colors. Very ornate but simple to copy

by making little rosettes of inch-wide picot-edged ribbon (they looked like marguerites). One edge of the ribbon was shirred so as to form a compact little disk, imitating the stamens of the flower, and the rosettes were ranged close beside each other, forming a double tier. A quaint stick-up motif, made of the same ribbon adorned the center front.

Petals and leaves are cut from velvet and caught to the hat with long stitches of dull blue wool

The revived interest in bead embroidery and chenille embroidery has resulted in an inexhaustible variety of really beautiful new trimming motifs, suitable for hats and matched sets. Particularly attractive are the ornaments suggesting the Far East, gorgeously colored Chinese, Japanese, Turkish, Persian and Indian designs, carried out in beads, metal flitters, lustrous silks and chenille. As intricate as these designs appear, they are copied with the greatest ease, for the beads and paillettes are easily applied, and in many instances it suffices to merely trace the pattern of a printed Eastern fabric.

Matched set (hat and reticule) trimmed with Grecian border in pink and blue French knots of silk. Beads may be substituted

No. 1
2 Lignes

No. 1½
3 Lignes

No. 2
4 Lignes

No. 3
6 Lignes

No. 4
8 Lignes

No. 5
10 Lignes

No. 7
13 Lignes

No. 9
17 Lignes

No. 12
21 Lignes

No. 16
25 Lignes

No. 22
30 Lignes

No. 30
32 Lignes

No. 40
35 Lignes

No. 50
37 Lignes

No. 60
40 Lignes

No. 80
45 Lignes

No. 100
50 Lignes

No. 120
54 Lignes

No. 200
60 Lignes

WIDTHS of MILLINERY RIBBONS
By NUMBER and LIGNE

In ordering ribbons always specify the width desired by its number. At the left of the illustrations are the standard numbers.

In the manufacture of ribbons and silks the Ligne is the unit in the measurement of the width. A ligne does not conform to any ordinary fraction of an inch, although as shown above, 12 lignes equal one and one-sixteenth ($1\frac{1}{16}''$) inches.

GLOSSARY OF RIBBON TERMS

Antique—An imitation of ribbons of other centuries.
Armure—A twilled weave showing a ribbed surface.
Bakst Designs—In the style of Leon Bakst, best known for his costume designs for the Russian Ballet. Barbaric, Oriental feeling expressed in a manner allied to Futurist. Crude forms in strong colors without shading—vigorous and sensuous.
Barré—Striped laterally, in same direction as the filling; similar to travers, showing transverse bars.
Basket Effect—An order of basket-like intersection of warp and weft, giving an enlarged hopsack appearance in the woven material, hence the special name.
Bayadere—striped horizontally, usually in alternating colors.
Bayadere Moiré—Same as above, with watered effect added.
Bébé Ribbon—The narrowest ribbon No. 1.
Bengaline de Soie—A plain, corded weave, resembling poplin, with warp and weft of silk.
Bouclé—French for buckled. A fabric with surface showing lock-of-hair effect.
Bouillonné—Having shirred or gathered effect.
Brocade—From the Spanish brocado, meaning brocaded or broché; from the Latin brocare, to prick, to figure. A heavy-weight silk with broché (raised) figures of flowers or foliage; in some instances with gold and silver threads interwoven. Any fabric woven in jacquard effect.
Brocatelle—A soft damask, having principal figures in raised effect.
Broché—A loom embroidered fabric woven with a figure.
Cachemire—(French for Cashmere or Kashmir). A style showing palms and other Persian and Indian patterns in dark, rich Oriental colorings. Akin to Persian effects.
Chameleon—Three-toned glacé effect.
Changeant—An effect produced by weaving two colors in a plain fabric.
Chiffonette—The flimsiest and most "bodiless" of all the chiffon family.
Chiffon-Taffeta—An exceedingly thin, soft, light-weight taffeta. The same will apply to all other weaves with the chiffon prefix.
Chiné—A warp print in blurred, indistinct design.
Comet—Same as bébé.
Damassé—With damask effects introduced. Applied to fabrics having a rich, heavy woven design similar to damask, which see.
Damier—A checkerboard pattern.
Dresden—Dainty flower design in imitation of Dresden china.
Epinglé—A ribbed fabric in vast variety, showing moderately large and smaller ribs alternating in plain, in figures and in colors.
Eponge—A French term for sponge cloth, or fabric of soft nubby yarns, also allied to terry-like weave effects.
Faille—A soft ribbed fabric without gloss.
Futurist Designs—Roughly drawn natural forms without shading. Colors diluted with white from sharp, hard colors, bringing them half-way between pastel tints and full-strength colors. Introduced as the style of the future, hence Futurist. Similar in principle to paintings of Futurist school.
Gauze—French, gaze, a very fine and peculiar weave of the bunting order. A thin voile, or veiling.
Glacé—A lustrous effect imparted by weaving two tones and special finish.
Grosgrain—A ribbed fabric, with heavy thread running crosswise.
Iridescent—Rainbow effect, showing prismatic hues.
Jardiniere—Conventional flower design in many colors.
Liberty Satin—A soft lustrous ribbon.
Lisse—On the gauze or chiffon order, with a crêpe twist.
Louisine—A fine-grained light-weight ribbon in invisible basket weave.
Lamé—Interwoven or edged with metallic thread or flitters.
Martine Designs—A large or small motif, often a flower and two or three leaves, is repeated at wide intervals on a plain background as an allover pattern. The drawing is purposely crude like the work of a child. There is no shading, coloring simple, originated in the Martine studio of Paul Poiret, the Paris couturier.
Matelassé—A weave showing a quilted effect, though on a very diminutive scale. From the French matelas; quilt.
Merveilleux—A satin showing a light lustrous twill.
Messaline—A finishing which may be applied to any weave, rendering it soft and simple.
Miroir—Mirror or looking-glass effect.
Moiré—Watered effect.
Moiré Antique—A fabric watered in antique effect.
Moiré Metallique—Representing watered, frosted and clouded effect. A metallic finish.
Moiré Nacré—Mother-of-pearl effect, showing the delicate pinkish flush and delicate tints seen in the interior of sea shells.
Moresque—Patterns or effects on the Moorish order.
Motif—The units of a design which is repeated over and over again in a pattern.
Nouveau—New. A novelty.
Ombré—A shaded effect by warping different tones.
Ottoman—On the order of faille, but coarser.
Panne—A new satin material de luxe.
Peau de Peche—Literally peach skin, having the soft touch like the skin of a peach.
Peau de Souris—Mouse skin, a soft finished silk not unlike duvetyn.
Peluche—Shaggy, rough, plush-like.
Pékiné—Fabrics in which the stripes, particularly of satin, run in the direction of the warp.
Persian Effects—Having the pattern of a cashmere shawl.
Picot—French for splinter. Applied to a pricked-out edge.
Pin Check—Minute squares of dots on the order of crossing hairlines.
Pointillé—Dotted.
Pompadour—Large floral design in soft colorings.
Post-Impressionist Designs—Natural forms simplified to give only impression of salient characteristics, not detail.
Radia—High, lustrous.
Rajah—Made of raw silk.

Rayé—Striped.
Repoussé—Pushed up. Pattern or design in raised effect.
Roman Stripe—A series of bright stripes of the same contrasting color or varying widths.
Satin—A silk, close texture and over short warp, which has a rich, glossy surface.
Scintillante—A changeable effect.

Taffeta Chameleon—Taffeta having two colors in the filling contrasting with a different one of the warp; a three-tone changeable effect.
Taffeta Metallique—A taffeta finished in metallic effect.
Tartan—From the French tartane; Spanish tiritana—a sort of thin silk. Also, a checkered or cross-pattern or plaid in colors such as are recognized as distinctive with the various Scottish clans.

Velours—Velvet.
Velours Epinglé—Velvet showing epingle or pin ribs.
Velours Grosgrain—A grosgrain weave with a rich, soft, velvet-like finish.
Velvet—A fabric either silk or cotton back, thick pile; erect threads.
Voiles—Veilings—The sheerest and thinnest of the hard twist gauze fabrics.

Index to Contents—The Art and Craft of Ribbon Work

A Guide for the Expert.   A Mentor for the Student.

Page

Art and Craft of Ribbon Work......... 7

Bags and Cases of Ribbon

Catch-All Bag......................... 61
Corset Bag............................ 54
Decorative Bag 50, 54
Folding Case 54
Hand Bags..................58, 59, 60, 61
Jewel Case 61
Needle Case 61
Pocket Work Case...................... 55
Sewing Bag (Sun Bonnet)............... 62
Work Bag 54
Work Case, Fitted..................... 61

Bows (For Corsage and Sash)

Aeroplane Bow 26
Matinee   "   41
Matron   "   41
Opera   "   41
Rosette   "   26
Sash   "   26

Bows (Hand Made)

Aeroplane Bow 48
Alsatian   " (Fancy)................. 25
Buckle   "   25
Butterfly   "   45
Cataract Bow 29
Coquette   "   25
Crescent   "   25
Dahlia   "   27
Diamond   "   45
Double Butterfly Bow.................. 48
Double Knot   "   45
Dragon Fly   "   43
Fancy Alsatian " 25, 49
Fancy Knotted   "   45
Fleur de Lys   "   43
Foliage   "   27
Ladder   "   43
Panache Bow 43
Poinsettia   "   45
Pyramid   "   44
Ribbon Chou 35
Spider   "   43
Tailored Ladder "   49
Tall Three-Loop Bow 19
Triple   "   47
Triple Alsatian Bow 23
Water Lily   "   48

Bows (Machine Made)

Aztec-Step Bow 39
Aster   "   31
Beetle   "   29
Butterfly   "   35
Checkerboard Bow 39
Chrysanthemum "   29
Cluster   "   32
Cockade   "   32
Cogwheel   "   39
Double Ring "   32
Drooping Loop "   29
Ear of Corn "   30
Erect   "   31
Fancy Loop "   29
Flat   "   30
Flower   "   30
Mercury   "   39
Meteor   "   29
Mitred Loop "   35
Picot   "   39
Pompon   "   39
Quill   "   35
Roll   "   35
Rose   "   39
Rosette   "   33
Seven End Tie "   39
Star   "   30

Page

Tie   Bow 39
Triple Dahlia " 29
Utility   " 39
Wing   " 34
Wreath   " 29

Braiding Ribbon

Braiding Ribbon (An effective way).... 22

Cockades

Buzz Saw 19
Cocarde 19-23
Legion d'honneur 19
Maltese Cross 18
Military Cockade 18
Nautical Star 18
Pin Wheel 19
Propeller 18

Feminine Finery

Breakfast Cap 54
Coiffure Band 54
Collar and Cuff Set................... 53
Corsage Ornaments 54
Flower Girdle and Wreath.............. 53
Girdle of Ribbon...................... 53
Neck Ruff " 53
Ribbon Boudoir Cap.................... 50
Ribbon Negligee 50
Sewing Apron 54

Flower Making; Lessons in

Lessons in Flower Making...14, 15, 16, 17
Chrysanthemum 14
Jonquil 17
Lily of English Crepe................. 17
Pansy 14
Poppy 14

Flowers of Ribbon (Ornamental)

Decorative Rose Bows.................. 11
Flower Boxes (for vanity flowers)...53, 61
Flower Girdle and Wreath.............. 53
Poinsettia Motif 23, 27
Ribbon Aster 31
Ribbon Calla Lily 11
Ribbon Carnation 37
Ribbon Chrysanthemum 29
Ribbon Dahlia 1, 27
Ribbon Hops 27
Ribbon Morning Glory.................. 21
Ribbon Rose Buds 11
Ribbon Rose Stick-Up 27
Ribbon Snowball 11
Ribbon Sunflower 37
Ribbon Water Lily 48
Vanity Flowers 52, 57
Violet Corsage 11

Gift Novelties

Brush and Buttonhook Holder.......... 54
Candle Shade 50
Foot Rest 50
Garter and Jewel Case................. 54
Hat Pin Holders....................55, 57
Individual Skirt Hangers.............. 54
Lamp Shade 50
Lingerie Ribbon Containers.........51, 54
Needle Book 51
Picture Frame 61
Pin Cushions 50, 51
Powder Puff and Box................51, 54
Ribbon Book Mark...................... 51
Ribbon Tambourin 51
Sachet Bags 55
Slipper Sole Puff 61
Strawberry Pincushion 45
Telephone Screen 50
Whisk Broom Holder.................... 57

Page

Gift Novelties for Babies

Baby Armlets 54
Baby Clothes Rack.................54, 57
Bonnet Stands 57
Clothes Hangers 57
Trinket Box 57

Hand Craft Motifs.................62, 63

Motifs and Ornaments

Buckle (Decorative).................. 23
Cabochon 23
Cone Motif 23
Cross   "   23
Dahlia   "   21
Daisy   "   23
Fabric Roses 21
Fruit Bud Ornament.................... 23
Inverted Pyramid Motif................ 27
Ornament 23
Ornamental Pin Motif.................. 23
Passion Flower   "   25
Pine Cone 36
Poinsettia Motif 24
Ribbon Hops 27
Ribbon Morning Glory.................. 21
Ribbon Plume 40
Rose Cabochon 21
Rose Cross 25
Rose Stick-Up 27
Spool Ornament (Tailored)............. 21
Star Motif 23
Toy Top 21
Wing Motif 19

Ornaments (Tailored) 46-47

Ornamental Bands (Machine Made)

Band Trimming 33
Crochet Band 33
Crown Garniture 31
Fancy Band 31
Hanging Loop Band..................... 32
Petal Band 31
Plaited Band 33
Zigzag Band 33

Ribbon Terms, Definitions, Measurements

Ribbon Terms, A Glossary of.......... 64

Rose Making; Lessons in

Applied Roses 10
Cherokee Rose 10
Fabric Roses from piece goods........ 10
Large Corsage Bouquet................. 10
Large Full Blown Rose.................. 8
Moss Rose Corsage Bow................. 10
Tiny Roses 10

Rosettes

Carnation Rosette 37
Cascade   "   44
Chrysanthemum Rosette 37
Conventional   " 21-23
Cross   "   19
Daisy   "   37
Double Rosette with Buds.............. 41
Flower Rosette 37
Petal Rosette 21
Pinwheel   "   21
Ribbon Dahlia Rosette................. 21
Ribbon Sunburst "   21
Rosette Bow 37
Sunflower Rosette 37
Twin Dahlia Rosette 23
Windmill   "   37

Widths of Millinery Ribbons 64

DIRECTIONS FOR MAKING TRIMMINGS

Ribbon Girdle

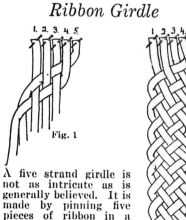

Fig. 1

Fig. 2

A five strand girdle is not as intricate as is generally believed. It is made by pinning five pieces of ribbon in a row, as in Fig. 1, and weaving them together by taking the fifth strand and laying it under the fourth, then over the third, under the second and over the first. Then begin weaving with the fourth strand, over and under the other strands, just as you did before, and repeat this, each time using the last strand at the right for the weaving. See Fig. 2.

Loop Braiding

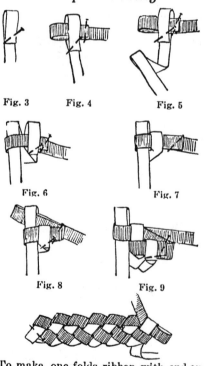

Fig. 3   Fig. 4   Fig. 5

Fig. 6   Fig. 7

Fig. 8   Fig. 9

To make, one folds ribbon with end on top and pins, Fig. 3. Another piece is similarly folded and pinned, always with top end up, and inserted end side up through the first loop, Fig. 4. The first ribbon is picked up as in Fig. 5 and inserted through loop of second ribbon, Fig. 6, pulled tightly into place. Ribbon number 2 is picked up as in Fig. 5 and run through second loop made by first ribbon, as in Fig. 7, continuing as in Figs. 8 and 9.

Diagonal Tucking

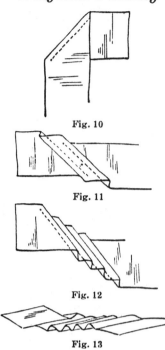

Fig. 10

Fig. 11

Fig. 12

Fig. 13

Interesting cocardes may be made by swirling this diagonally tucked ribbon. Belting or grosgrain ribbon may be used. Fold as in Fig. 10, make one-quarter inch tucks on bias one-quarter inch apart, Fig. 11, continuing as in Fig. 12. Fig. 13 shows the reverse side.

In this manner the time for making the flat rose is materially lessened.

When a large flower for a hat is desired one of the large double-headed hat pins is used. Wider ribbon, treated in the same manner, as above, will produce excellent results.

The pin is not withdrawn. A large flower of this kind can be made within a half minute.

The Three-minute Flower

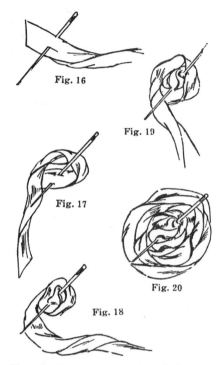

Fig. 16

Fig. 19

Fig. 17

Fig. 20

Fig. 18

Here is the exact opposite of the century plant. Far from requiring a hundred years to burst into blossom, this flower takes but three minutes at the most.

Flat flowers for ornamenting pillows, boudoir accessories, baby things, lingerie and frocks are made very simply—in this fashion.

Instead of laboriously twisting a piece of ribbon in the fingers to get a small rose or rosette, one may now, as quick as a wink, make an entire flower by taking a long needle and catching one end of the ribbon to the material which is to be decorated with the flower, as in Fig. 16. The ribbon is then twisted underneath the two ends of the needle, as illustrated in Figs. 17, 18, 19 and 20. The entire operation of twisting the ribbon underneath the needle should only take a few seconds. Another needle which has been threaded is used to tack down this flower, wherever it is deemed necessary, to gain the desired results.

Four-petaled Flower

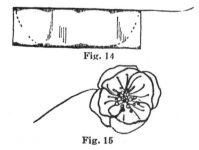

Fig. 14

Fig. 15

Four petals are stitched as in Fig. 14 and drawn together with stamens in center as in Fig. 15.

HOW TO FASHION VARIOUS FLOWERS

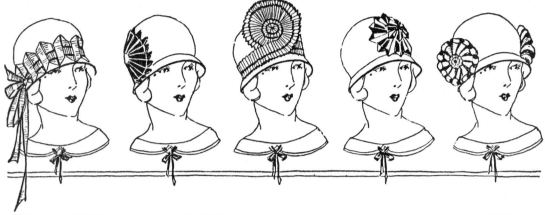

Five Ways of Trimming the Same Hat

Ribbon is the Crowning Glory of the Cloche Shape

Many ingenious women use the one hat for varied occasions, changing its identity by snapping on or pinning on different ribbon trimmings to carry out the color scheme or the spirit of the costume.

HAT 1.
Fold ribbon as shown in Figs. 1 and 2 and run a contrasting ribbon through every other fold as indicated in Fig. 2.

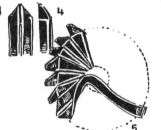

HAT 2.
Fold ribbon as illustrated in Fig. 3 and then as in Fig. 4 and sew on a buckram foundation around in a circle as in Fig. 5.

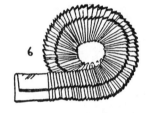

HAT 3.
A piece of five-inch ribbon is folded over so that there is an inch of the lower piece showing. Have it side pleated and swirl it into a circle, as in Fig. 6. Finally, take one-half yard of two-inch ribbon and fold the same way into a smaller rosette for the center.

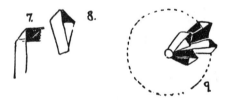

HAT 4.
A cocarde is made by twisting two-tone ribbon as illustrated in Figs. 7 and 8. The ribbon is laid to show the two shades alternately light and dark, as in Fig. 9.

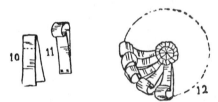

HAT 5.
This trimming is made by folding over a piece of wristwatch ribbon or ribbon slightly wider, placing an almost invisible tuck a half inch from the top of each loop, as in Figs. 10 and 11, then arrange the loops into a complete circle, as in Fig. 12.

Ribbon Strip for Petal,
Showing Stitching

Morning Glory

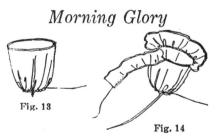

Fig. 13

Fig. 14

Morning glories add their loveliness to a graceful spray or a wreath. The ribbon is cut, sewn together and gathered at base as in Fig. 13. A narrow ribbon is gathered and sewn to edge, and flower drawn up as in Fig. 14.

Wild Rose

Roses form an effective trimming, and are easily made. The stamens around which the petals are placed may be purchased in a millinery supply department.

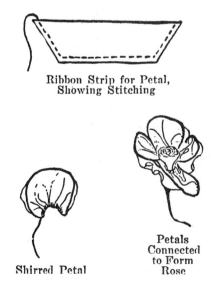

Shirred Petal

Petals
Connected
to Form
Rose

EASY-TO-FOLLOW INSTRUCTIONS

Shirring and Plaiting

Diagram 1. Ribbon shirred through center.
Requires 1½ times as much material as covered space.

Diagram 2. Ribbon ruffled at one selvage.
Twice amount of ribbon as covered space.

Diagram 3. Triangle to give pointed effect.
Twice as much material as space to be covered.

Diagram 4. Ribbon side plaited for ruffle.
Use twice as much material as space covered.

Diagram 5. Ribbon plaited in honey-comb effect.
Use twice as much ribbon as space to be covered. Very effective trimming.

Lattice Work of Ribbon and Lace. Pointed Ends of Ribbon

Many articles of decoration or wearing apparel need only the above variation for trimming. The lace runs crosswise and the ribbon up and down, overlapping to form a point.

Rosettes or Single Bows Easily Made

Twist on Fingers or Parallel Bars

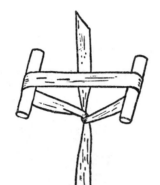

Single Bow in Process of Knotting

Rosette Made as in Process 3

Twist Ribbon Around Many Times for Rosette

Single Bow as in Process 2

Simple Leaf

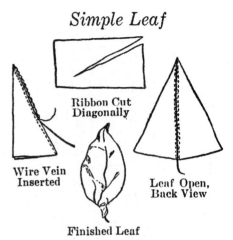

Ribbon Cut Diagonally

Wire Vein Inserted

Leaf Open, Back View

Finished Leaf

This type of leaf is very easily made and may be used with practically all the ribbon flowers shown in this book, if one desires.

Diagonal Stitching

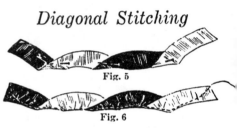

Fig. 5

Fig. 6

Diagonal stitching done on two-tone ribbon. The ribbon is folded as in Fig. 5, gathered as in Fig. 6, and drawn up to form black and white flower

Petal

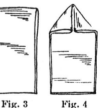

Fig. 3   Fig. 4

Many exquisite flowers and ornaments may be made from these petals, one of which is shown in ornament on page 19 especially good for dahlia and asters. The ribbon is folded as in Fig. 3, corners turned over as in Fig. 4, and base gathered.

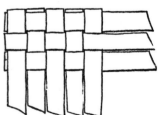

Lattice Work of Ribbon. Ribbon Running Lengthwise and Crosswise

This is a simple form of decoration and is worked in the same manner as the lattice to the left. The crown of a hat, pillow, etc., may be decorated in this charming fashion.

WITHOUT TAKING ONE STITCH

The above cocarde is developed in two-tone satin ribbon 1 inch wide mounted on a circle of buckram 5 inches in diameter. 12 pieces of ribbon 3½ inches long are cut. Two pieces of 1-inch metallic ribbon are laid on the buckram to form a cross; the ends are turned down over the rim of the buckram and firmly lepaged underneath. Three pieces of ribbon, selvedges touching, are lepaged to the wrong side of the circle, drawn over the edge to the right side, the left edge of each turned back and drawn to a point.

Charming rosettes can easily be made from metallic ribbon by twisting it and pinching it into place as shown in the three lower figures. It is then fashioned into circles and lightly lepaged to a background of crinoline. Colors such as rose and old blue may be combined, as was done in the original of the illustration. This motif may be varied indefinitely for trimming lace and chiffon dresses, lampshades and novelties.

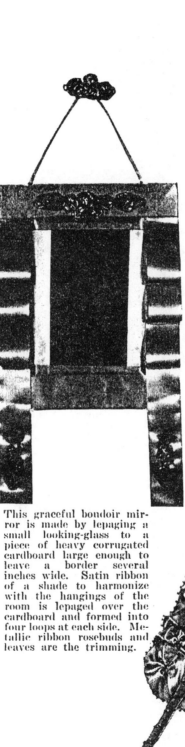

This graceful boudoir mirror is made by lepaging a small looking-glass to a piece of heavy corrugated cardboard large enough to leave a border several inches wide. Satin ribbon of a shade to harmonize with the hangings of the room is lepaged over the cardboard and formed into four loops at each side. Metallic ribbon rosebuds and leaves are the trimming.

To make rosebuds of metallic ribbon, tie five knots, one after the other as shown in figures 1 to 6. Then fashion into a small circle (figure 7) and fasten the ends with a bit of glue. The leaves are made by twisting a bit of ribbon as in figure 9. Then bend the two ends together and fasten with glue as in figure 8.

Tiny circles of picot ribbon gathered on their own picot thread and attached to a background of heavy crinoline form this effective ribbon plume for hat or gown. The stem is made from a piece of whalebone wrapped with ribbon and fixed firmly to the background.

GAY GARTERS ARE THE VOGUE

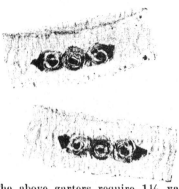

These simple garters are made of 1¼ yards of 1½-inch grosgrain ribbon and 1 yard of 1-inch colored ribbon, sewed as in Diagram I. Decorate with large plaited wheel, another small one of contrasting color, and a tiny metal buckle. The cockades on the slippers above require: 1 yard of 1-inch grosgrain ribbon. Make ¼-inch plaits, forming wheel of 3-inch diameter. 2 streamers 2½ inches long trim each cockade. A metal buckle is placed in center.

The above garters require 1⅓ yards of 2-inch figured ribbon for the foundation, 2⅔ yards of ½-inch satin ribbon for the under side of garter; allowing ¼ inch on each side, sew as in Diagram II. Decorate with 3 buds.

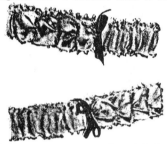

These garters are made with 1 yard of 1½-inch 2-tone ribbon, and the same amount of 1-inch ribbon of contrasting color, sewed as in Diagram I. Decorate with 4 petals and bow.

Black satin ribbon edged with a metallic ribbon with three bows of the metallic ribbon is used in this garter. ⅝ yard 1-inch ribbon for each garter, 1⅜ yards of ⅜-inch for edging and bows.

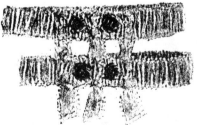

Diagram I. Ribbon of different widths. Narrower ribbon placed to form right side or under side.

Diagram II. Under side, showing ribbon placed for narrow elastic on top and bottom.

Diagram III. Ribbons of same width, allowing for ruffling on top and bottom.

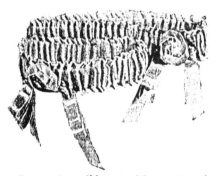

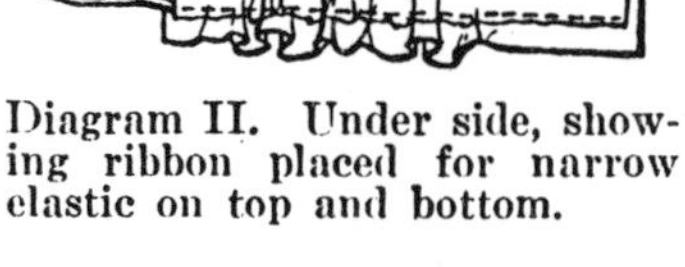

Grosgrain ribbon with contrasting edges makes a unique garter. ⅝ yard of 1¼-inch ribbon is needed for each garter, and 1¼ yard ½-inch for trimming. For rose details, see page 26.

The picot-edge ribbon garters above require ⅝ yard of 1-inch ribbon for each garter; 1½ yards of ½ inch for knotted ends; 4 inches ½ inch for each rose, and 3 inches ¼ inch for leaves.

Metallic picot ribbon edged with ¼-inch velvet ribbon and lace. ⅝ yard 1-inch metallic picot ribbon is needed for each garter, ⅝ yard ¼-inch velvet ribbon for edging and ⅝ yard for bow knot, and ¾ yard of lace.

For flower details see pages 66 and 80

A COCARDE AND ITS VARIATIONS

A

A—Make center of above cocarde exactly like Fig. B, then between each pointed petal place a loop of contrasting ribbon. Very striking color combinations can be achieved in this cocarde suitable for frock or hat.

The steps used in making the cocardes on this page are the foundation of nearly all cocardes.

D—Process of making this dainty trimming is exactly the same as that employed in the first five steps of Fig. B. Cocarde is turned face backward, as indicated in Fig. 6: the inner and outer points are laid one over the other and tacked together, forming one center circle through which a piece of ribbon is drawn and knotted as illustrated.

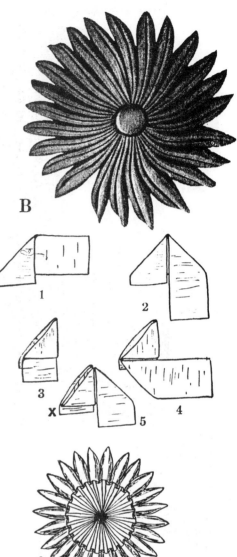

B

1 **2** **3** **4** **X** **5**

6

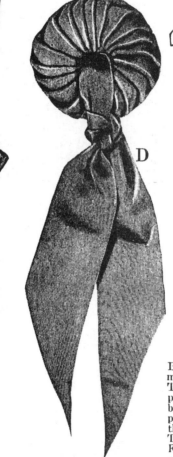

C

D

E—Is exactly the same as B, excepting that every other petal-point is folded in toward the center and tacked.

E

C—Details for making this effective cocarde are the same as illustrated for B. Turn finished cocarde so that the back becomes the front as indicated in Fig. 6. Tack the outer points into a small circle. Draw a ribbon through these two circles, and place a knot over the upper one, as indicated in illustration.

B—The rosette above is as easy to make as it is charming when completed. Take ribbon 1½ inches wide or wider, preferably grosgrain, and after making bias folds as indicated in Figs. 1 and 2, place the right-hand bias immediately over the left-hand bias as indicated in Fig. 3. This gives the first petal of the cocarde. Fold the remaining portion of the ribbon at right angles as indicated in Fig. 4 to form another bias and lay the third bias over the second. Then repeat the first step as indicated in Fig. 5, again laying the right-hand bias over the left-hand bias, which gives two petals. When these two petals are done, start tacking at the inner points where the petals meet, indicated by letter X in Fig. 5, and begin the third petal as indicated in Fig. 4, repeating until 24 petals are done. Finish center, where points are connected, with self-covered button. Of 1½-inch ribbon, 2 yards are required for a 24-petal cocarde. Of 2-inch ribbon, 4 inches are required for each petal.

PARIS SENDS THESE BOWS AND COCARDES

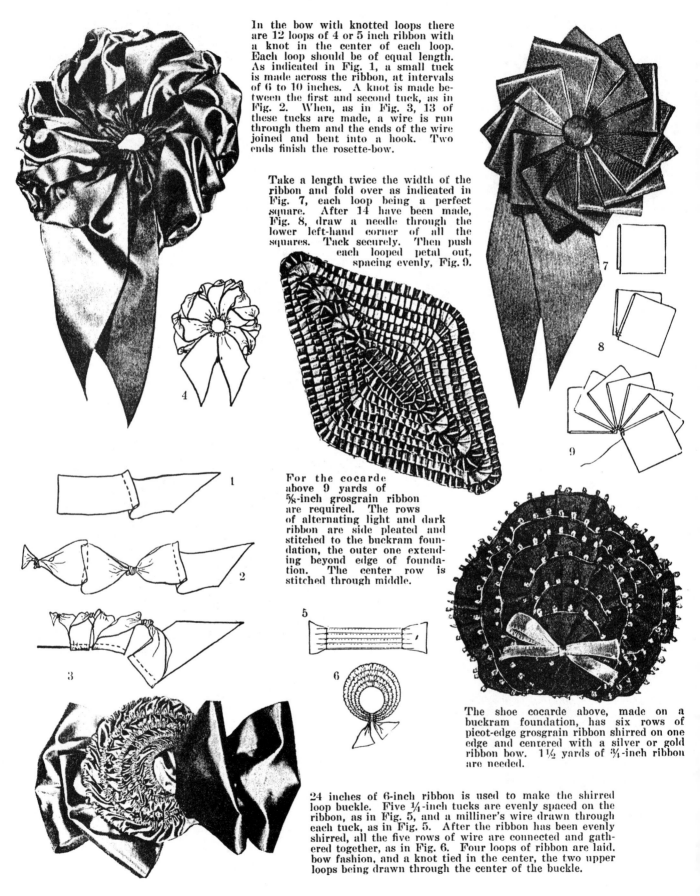

In the bow with knotted loops there are 12 loops of 4 or 5 inch ribbon with a knot in the center of each loop. Each loop should be of equal length. As indicated in Fig. 1, a small tuck is made across the ribbon, at intervals of 6 to 10 inches. A knot is made between the first and second tuck, as in Fig. 2. When, as in Fig. 3, 13 of these tucks are made, a wire is run through them and the ends of the wire joined and bent into a hook. Two ends finish the rosette-bow.

Take a length twice the width of the ribbon and fold over as indicated in Fig. 7, each loop being a perfect square. After 14 have been made, Fig. 8, draw a needle through the lower left-hand corner of all the squares. Tack securely. Then push each looped petal out, spacing evenly, Fig. 9.

For the cocarde above 9 yards of ⅝-inch grosgrain ribbon are required. The rows of alternating light and dark ribbon are side pleated and stitched to the buckram foundation, the outer one extending beyond edge of foundation. The center row is stitched through middle.

The shoe cocarde above, made on a buckram foundation, has six rows of picot-edge grosgrain ribbon shirred on one edge and centered with a silver or gold ribbon bow. 1½ yards of ¾-inch ribbon are needed.

24 inches of 6-inch ribbon is used to make the shirred loop buckle. Five ¼-inch tucks are evenly spaced on the ribbon, as in Fig. 5, and a milliner's wire drawn through each tuck, as in Fig. 5. After the ribbon has been evenly shirred, all the five rows of wire are connected and gathered together, as in Fig. 6. Four loops of ribbon are laid, bow fashion, and a knot tied in the center, the two upper loops being drawn through the center of the buckle.

"BEAUTY'S BROW IS RIBBON WREATHED"

The front of ornament is made of ribbon petals with a center of ¼-inch silver ribbon swirled. 5 yards of two-toned ribbon are required; ¾ yard ¼-inch metallic ribbon knotted in center; and 1 yard 5½-inch satin ribbon, pastel shade, to cover front and back of buckram foundation. See Petal, page 68.

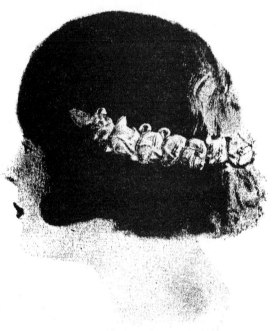

Folded silver ribbon makes this classic laurel wreath with side rosettes of loops. 2½ yards of ¾-inch ribbon are needed. The folded loops are sewn on a ribbon band.

A shirred ribbon head-band requires 27 inches of 2-inch ribbon and 4 inches of ½-inch scalloped ribbon for each flower.

Bits of brilliant coloring adeptly placed against dark backgrounds are considered a necessary touch on the smart Parisienne's costume. 1½ yards 3-inch grosgrain ribbon is needed for this lovely poppy. The petals varying in size are cut as indicated on page 78, rolled at sides, gathered top and bottom and placed around a silk pompon. Contrast is gained by a spray of delicate foliage.

Twenty-seven inches of 2-inch gold ribbon makes this bandeau requiring 2 yards of ⅜-inch metallic ombre ribbon for flowers, and 5 inches of ½-inch metallic ribbon for each leaf.

For bobbed locks there is this lovely band of rose and silver. 2½ yards of ⅜-inch silver ribbon are required for leaves and 2½ yards of 1-inch rose ombre for flowers.

COCARDES THAT ARE NEW AND SMART

A cocarde that is original and smart is the one on the left, made on a fan-shaped buckram foundation. The entire cocarde is made of alternating rows of ribbon loops and side pleated ribbon. Three pieces of ribbon, each differing 1 inch in length, are folded one over the other and placed at center for a finish. 4½ yards of 1¼-inch ribbon are needed for the entire cocarde. ¼ yard 5-inch satin ribbon is needed to cover the foundation.

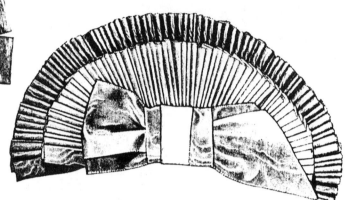

The coquettish fan ornament makes an equally charming finish for the modish cloche or the wide hat brim of plush or velvet. The buckram foundation is a semi-circle, measuring 6 inches across. One yard of 3-inch ribbon is pleated on to the outer edge of the foundation and ¾ yard of 2-inch ribbon makes the inner semi-circle. ½ yard is needed for the bow that finishes the center.

Fig. 2

These quaint flowers made of the new scalloped ombre (shaded) ribbons seem almost to gather themselves into such bewitching blossoms, Fig. 3. The center is a narrow piece of ribbon joined at the ends and gathered at the bottom, with scant gathers at the top to form the tiny nest for the stamens, Fig. 2. 1 yard of ½-inch scalloped ribbon required for each flower.

Fig. 3

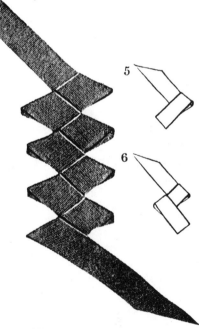

5

6

Fig. 1

The wheel cocarde, left, is sponsored by the exclusive woman everywhere. One may make it easily at home, confident that it has all the loveliness of those in the best shops. 4½ yards of 1-inch ribbon are folded into 9-inch lengths as in Fig. 1, then folded again as in Fig. 2. The pieces are then arranged in wheel fashion on a buckram foundation.

Fig. 2

This is a very effective trimming for a dress or hat. Fold a piece of ribbon as indicated in Fig. 5, and tack. Then reverse the loop as indicated in Fig. 6, tack again, forming a double diamond shape. The process is repeated as many times as required for the length of trimming needed. Several widths of ribbon are suitable, but the ½-inch width in grosgrain is preferable.

CLEVER AND COLORFUL TRIMMINGS

6

7

C—A very smart yet simple trimming is made by gathering 3 inches of ⅜-inch ribbon to form a circle ⅜ inch in diameter as indicated in Fig. 6 to the left. A ribbon is drawn through the rings over the seams as in Fig. 7. In tacking this ribbon on to the material which it will trim, steel beads may be used along the outer edges.

Ombre shaded ribbon lends itself especially to this many sided cocarde made of ten 3-inch strips of ribbon, alternating with loops made as in Fig. 4. The center of the motif is made with several single short loops and pointed ends, Fig. 3.

Fig. 3

Fig. 4

Fig. 1

Naïve petals hold their secret well in this flower cocarde, but even secrets may be told when they hold so much loveliness that might be shared. The petals of two-tone ribbon turn just a bit of the inner edge out as in Fig. 1 and the edges of the inner color brought together, overlapped and gathered and arranged in four rows on a foundation, beginning at outer edge. The tiny bud at the center is a bit of twisted ribbon, see page 66. 4 yards of 1-inch two-tone ribbon are required for this effective cocarde.

C

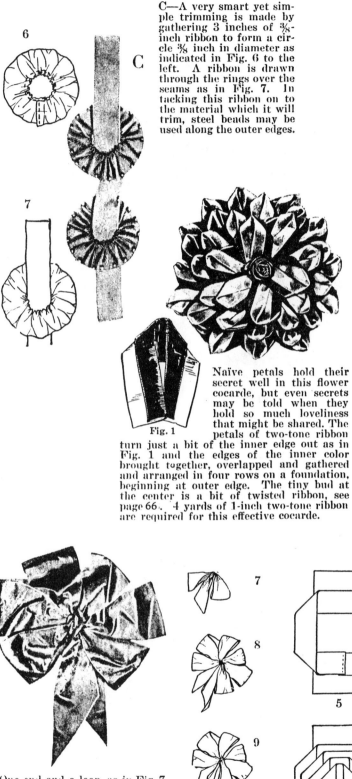

7

8

9

5

6

One end and a loop, as in Fig. 7, are wound with several strands of thread to hold them securely. Five additional loops are each fastened in the same manner, as in Fig. 8. The remaining end of ribbon is drawn between loops three and four, and is knotted on the reverse side, as in Fig. 9, the remaining end being cut the same length as the first end. Both ends are cut on the bias.

C—A wide piece of ribbon is used for a foundation. 1-inch ribbon is laid in the form of a square with the corners biased as indicated in Fig. 5. The inner rows are laid over as indicated in Fig. 6, each row a separate piece of ribbon. Cover stitches with button and two ends, as illustrated.

NEW HATS AND THE TRIMMINGS THEY FANCY

Fig. 1

This ribbon quill of moire ribbon is made by cutting graduated pieces of ribbon folded as in Fig. 1 and placed one upon the other on a quill-shaped piece of buckram wired at edges and through center. 3 yards ¾-inch shaded ombre ribbon are needed and 11 inches of 3-inch satin ribbon for lining.

Colorful satin ribbon with corded edge, faced with a metallic ribbon, is caught 1 inch below edge of brim, turned diagonally over to show the metal color and caught on under side of brim. The crown is made entirely of alternating rows of ribbon radiating from the center. The hat is made over buckram shape and requires 8 yards each of 1¼-inch ribbons.

The collapsible mousquetaire ribbon hat above is of heavy satin back moire ribbon 8 inches wide. The brim requires 38 inches with dart at middle front. For the crown 25 inches are required. The 9 darts measure 3 inches at selvedge, Fig. 1 (A-B), 4½ inches, selvedge to point (C). Darts brought together inside crown, Fig. 2. Brim 38 inches of ribbon with darts in middle front wired. 2 inches turned under wired band, Fig. 3. Pleats on sides give necessary flare. Lines (D-E) and (F-G), Fig. 4, show where ribbon is folded one end over other and finished with cocarde.

See page 80 for working diagram.

The girdle, bag and hat cocarde on figure above are of novelty edged grosgrain ribbon. The ribbon is simply gathered along one edge and folded in a zig-zag way to give the pleated effect.

FOR THE COSTUME FASHIONABLE

The wheel-fancy at left, with long wide streamers, makes a charming finish for a simple one-piece or draped frock. 5 yards of 2-inch ribbon are required for the wheel.

The vestee with Peter Pan collar is made entirely of ribbon. 1¼ yards of 9-inch fancy ribbon makes the vest, and 1½ yards of 8-inch plain ribbon is used for Peter Pan collar. The opening at the neck is trimmed with blanket stitches of baby ribbon.

Pieces of ribbon unevenly folded and sewn to foundation make this girdle with many streamers. For flower at center, see pages 66 and 67. The motif requires 4 yards of ½-inch ribbon.

The wide crushed girdle below is given a front motif made of ribbon wrapped wire and a ribbon flower. The bow is made of loops with one looped streamer and pointed end.

Six loops of ribbon with turned back corners and pointed streamers.

The cocarde shown on right is made of 1 yard of 1½-inch belting ribbon with ¼-inch bias tucks. For details of bias tuckings, see page 28. When series of ½-inch tucks have been made ribbon is swirled round and round to make flower effect.

This fetching hat requires 15 yards of ¾-inch two-tone ribbon. Cut into lengths measuring the height of crown and width of brim of frame to be covered. The pieces are folded through center on bias, as in Fig. 1 on page 76, and the center of the fold placed on edge of brim with one piece placed over the other until brim and side of crown are covered. The top of the crown is covered by similarly folded pieces with half light ends and half dark ends showing and arranged as in quill on page 76.

A BOUQUET OF RIBBON FLOWERS

When one has learned to make this simple rose petal, roses may be made in an endless variety. A piece of ribbon is folded in half and gathered at the bottom. The corner of each loop is turned back as in Figs. 3 and 4. The first petal is rolled spirally and each successive petal partially surrounds the preceding petal, until a bud or full rose is formed. Stem and calyx are added. The size of rose desired can always be regulated by the width of the ribbon used. Ribbon 2 inches wide makes one the actual size of an American Beauty Rose.

Fig. 11

These delicately colored wistaria petals lend an interesting touch to pillows, negligees or lampshades. They may be used singly or together for girdles, hatbands, or merely as decorative motifs. 3 inches of 1-inch satin edged taffeta ribbon are needed for each petal. The ribbon is gathered as in Fig. 11, drawn up and wired as in Fig. 12. The stem is wrapped with floss.

Fig. 12

4

3

These are back views of petal.

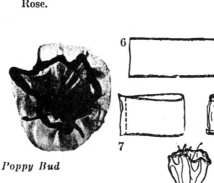

Poppy Bud

6

7   8

9

A piece of ribbon, as in Fig. 6, either with a black edge woven in the ribbon, or a narrow black ribbon edge attached, is folded and seamed as in Fig. 7. This loop of ribbon is turned inside out, to hide the seam. It is then gathered top and bottom as in Fig. 8 and the lower gather pulled in tightly around a stem to which the stamens have been attached. A dozen of these flowers makes an effective corsage.

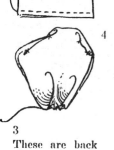

Fig. 2

Fig. 3

A youthful hat or gown may go gayly forth adorned with these dainty berry-like flowers. 4 inches of 1½-inch ribbon are required for each flower. These are cut and seamed as in Fig. 2, and turned inside out so that raw edges do not show; stamens inserted and the ribbon gathered at top as in Fig. 3. The flower is then stuffed with bits of cotton gathered at the bottom and shaped to resemble a berry. Leaf detail on page 68.

Petals of varying size, cut as in Fig. 3, rolled at side and gathered top and bottom as in Figs. 4 and 5, are placed around a full group of stamens. Connect the base of the petals to a stem, and cover the connection with a calyx. This flower is easy to make, and the results most gratifying.

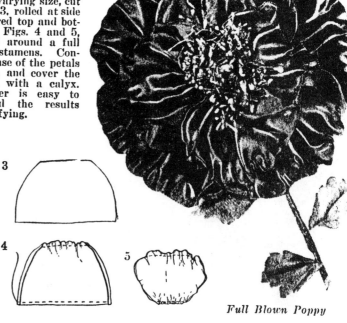

3

4   5

Full Blown Poppy

FROM PETAL TO FULL BLOOM

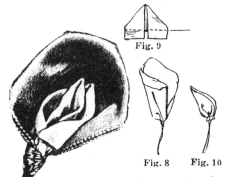

Fig. 9

Fig. 8   Fig. 10

Fig. 4   Fig. 5

Corsages of exquisitely colored sweet peas are both graceful and modish. 3 inches of 1½-inch ribbon makes the outer petal and 3 inches of ⅝-inch ribbon the centers of these blossoms. Ribbon for petal is folded in half, corners folded under and held with stitches, as in Fig. 8, bottom shirred and drawn up tightly. The centers are folded, as in Fig. 9, shirred at bottom, folded in half and gathered, as in Fig. 10. Green floss covered wire makes stem.

Simplicity is the password one must use to be admitted to fashion's realms and this flower motif on chapeaux or frocks will readily gain one an entree. 2½ inches of ½-inch ombre ribbon makes each petal. The ribbon is folded as in Fig. 4, gathered at the bottom and wired as in Fig. 5. The stem is wrapped with green floss.

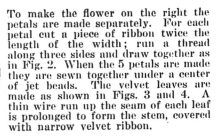

Fig. 2

Fig. 3   Fig. 4

To make the flower on the right the petals are made separately. For each petal cut a piece of ribbon twice the length of the width; run a thread along three sides and draw together as in Fig. 2. When the 5 petals are made they are sewn together under a center of jet beads. The velvet leaves are made as shown in Figs. 3 and 4. A thin wire run up the seam of each leaf is prolonged to form the stem, covered with narrow velvet ribbon.

Fig. 6   Fig. 7

For the small hat, this quaint posy is well liked. It is made by using ¾-inch scalloped ombre ribbon, appliqued on to a stamped design, thus giving a flat, yet soft, flower. The leaves are made by folding 6 inches of green metallic ribbon into squares and sewing into place on material. One may work out many other designs in this way, either originating the pattern or transferring it.

This many petaled flower requires 3 inches of ⅞-inch ribbon for each inner petal and 4 inches for outer. The petals are made as in Fig. 6. The 14 outer petals, sewed in a circle right to left, form a foundation for the 11 inner petals, which are lapped from left to right, as in Fig. 7, under each other around stamens. The stem is wrapped with floss and finished with calyx.

DETAILS AND DIAGRAMS OF ARTICLES SHOWN ON OTHER PAGES

Bag on Page 81

An original handbag developed in ½-inch red moire combined with black novelty ribbon patterned in red, gold and green. It is 7 inches wide and 5½ inches deep. On a foundation of silk the ribbon is applied in lines as illustrated, leaving enough to extend beyond the foundation to form a fringe at the lower edge. Bones are run through a casing at the top. The lining is of 7-inch red taffeta ribbon.

Flat Purse on Page 81

It is developed in navy and red plisse ribbon latticed. It requires 8½ yards of ¾-inch ribbon and 1 yard of 7-inch ribbon for lining and pocket.

Directions for Making Flat Purse

Take 2 pieces of canvas 16 inches long and slightly less than 7 inches wide; join with rows of stitching for firmness. Lay canvas on ribbon for outside of purse and turn over ½-inch on canvas at each end. Cut a piece of crinoline same size as canvas and cover with lining ribbon. If pockets are desired they should be stitched to lining at this stage. Pin outside and lining together and either stitch both together on the very edge or overcast with fine stitches. Turn up 5 inches, and on each end and insert wedges. These, when finished, should be 5 inches deep and 3 inches wide at top and are made of the outside and lining ribbons.

The outside and lining pieces for the wedges are basted together with all edges turned in, then a wedge is inserted on each side and overcast with very fine stitches to the body of the purse. One large snap fastener may be used to fasten the flap to the purse; or two snap fasteners may be preferred, one a little bit in from each corner.

Working Diagram of Hat Shown on Page 76

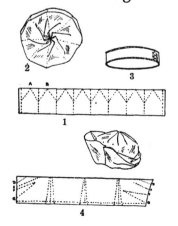

Rosebud

When making the bud, the ribbon may be used in one of two ways: either by folding double and making the fold the upstanding edge, or using a ribbon with a heavy edge or selvedge. Whichever is used, the details are the same. The ribbon is first twisted spirally as in Figs. 5 and 6 and continues to wind spirally. When a bud or rose of the size desired is obtained, the ribbon is pulled down toward the stem, as in Fig. 7 and tied with thread.

The corsage above is of rose satin ribbon, combined with rose ombre metallic plissé and green metallic plissé for leaves. Seven inches are required for each leaf (see page 30 for directions for leaf). On a circle of crinoline are mounted 2 rows of petals (see page 30 for petals) requiring 2¼ yards of 6-inch ribbon and 1¼ yards of 1⅛-inch rose ombre ribbon for central petals of flower.

Detail of Button

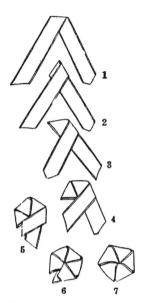

Fold ribbon as in Fig. 1. Then bring right-hand ribbon over left-hand ribbon, Fig. 2. Again bring right hand ribbon over left to form Fig. 3. Repeat 3 times, Figs. 4, 5 and 6. Then draw ribbon together, tack end under other side, Fig. 7.

The trimming of the hat above is developed in blue 2½-inch grosgrain ribbon combined with Roman striped ribbon 1½ inches wide. Directions given for Fig. B on page 30 may be followed for making the several groups of pointed petals. The striped ribbon is loosely knotted in the front and on the sides and attached to the foundation. The ends form a band in the back. 2¾ yards of 2½ inch grosgrain and 3¾ yards of Roman stripe are required.

ORIGINALITY IN RIBBON ACCESSORIES

The sports band is designed for bobbed hair. The ribbon ends back of the ear on either side and is there attached to ½-inch wide elastic which passes under the hair in the back. 1¼ yards of ribbon from 5 to 7 inches wide are required.

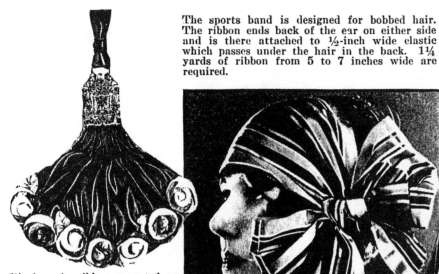

Black satin ribbon mounted on a silver top with roses of ombre metallic plissé ribbon shading from pale pink to deep rose. Green metallic plissé ribbon leaves.

In the large bow worn on the side at the hip line and especially designed for the one-piece frock we have one of the most attractive of the season's newest accessories. The wide Roman stripe here used is very smart, but many plain and double-faced ribbons will prove equally so. It is made with two loops and one end finished with a knotted fringe of crochet silk. 1⅛ yards of 6- or 8-inch ribbon and one spool of crochet silk are required.

The draped hat on the left is developed in 6¼-inch black satin-faced grosgrain ribbon mounted on an unwired turban shape of crinoline. On the left side the ends of four pieces of ribbon are sewn. These are draped over the hat, covering the crinoline surface and are fastened on the right side, with two ends reaching to the shoulder.

The scarf above is made of two lengths of soft ribbon 2⅓ yards long. One is navy blue, the other a soft, golden orange. The binding and trimming bands are 2½-inch white grosgrain. Blue and orange crochet silk are combined in the knotted fringe. The small hat is trimmed with 2½-inch white grosgrain ribbon laid in cartridge pleats, ending in a flat tailored bow in back. The cartridge pleats should be tacked to a foundation band first.

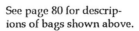

See page 80 for descriptions of bags shown above.

1. Wide Jacquard forms the center of this bag, with navy blue Satin de Luxe ribbon stitched in grey extending from either side.

2. This bag is made from wide Jacquard ribbon in a novelty shape; there is no other trimming used.

3. Wide Faille ribbon forms the ground of this bag. The pleated narrow Democracy gros grain ribbon made to form wheels. The two ribbons used are in contrasting colors.

4. A wide Jacquard ribbon is the body of this bag. A navy blue Satin de Luxe ribbon in a narrow width is used to make the edging. Novelty green gold frame, with narrow Satin de Luxe ribbon as a handle.

5. A navy blue and gold Jacquard ribbon makes this effective opera bag, with little bud trimmings of jackrose Satin de Luxe ribbon.

6. This parachute frame hand bag is made of a fancy ribbon and wide henna Satin de Luxe combined.

7. A combination of navy blue Satin de Luxe ribbon and blue and grey Jacquard makes this bag a novelty.

8. Handkerchief case made of Satin de Luxe ribbon. The small buds are made of Satin de Luxe ribbon to represent forget-me-nots.

9. Traveling kit. Made of Satin de Luxe ribbon in delft blue shades, set off with variegated flower trimmings.

10. Collapsible coat hanger built on metal frame and covered with Satin de Luxe ribbon.

11. Jewel box is covered with jackrose satin and narrow Pivoine shirred to form petals.

12. Doll pin cushion made from Satin de Luxe in lavender. Narrow ribbon for decoration.

13. Handkerchief case made of two shades of old rose Sankanac ribbon. A doll's head surmounts the top and is surrounded by wide ruffle with narrow satin ribbon around the body of the doll.

The Seven Ages of Ribbons

SHAKESPEARE IN HIS SEVEN AGES DIVIDED LIFE INTO DISTINCT TYPES, INTO CHARACTERS SO VIVID THAT IN DESCRIBING THEM, HE GAVE A PICTURE OF LIFE AS A WHOLE.

AS THESE PAGES UNFOLD YOU WILL FIND "THE SEVEN AGES OF RIBBON"— THE DISTINCT TYPES OF LOVELY FEMININITY FOR WHOSE BEAUTY AND ADORNMENT RIBBON MAKING HAS BECOME ONE OF THE CHIEF ARTS. BUT, IF YOU THINK FOR A MOMENT YOU WILL REALIZE THAT THE "SEVEN AGES" GIVE A SERIES OF PICTURES PORTRAYING THE FEMININE LIFE IN ITS ENTIRETY, FOR THERE IS NOT AN HOUR IN HER LIFE THAT WOMAN CANNOT BE MADE MORE BEAUTIFUL BY THE USE OF RIBBON, ELSEWHERE DESCRIBED AS THE CHOSEN DAUGHTER OF SILK.

SO, GRACIOUSLY PERMIT US TO INTRODUCE TO YOU THE SEVEN AGES OF RIBBON, STARTING ON THIS PAGE WITH CHILDHOOD.

Childhood. This dress is made of fine batiste, combined with valenciennes lace and insertings. Ribbon rosebuds and rosettes that decorate the dress are made of pale pink Trousseau ribbon.

Child's bonnet, crown is made of net finely tucked, narrow Trousseau ribbon in pale pink criss-crossed over net. Narrow silk lace and Trousseau ribbon ruffled together to form brim, which is faced with white straw. There are rosebud decorations of contrasting colors.

Princess slip made of fine batiste, combined with narrow valenciennes lace and beading. Pale pink Trousseau ribbon used for rosettes.

This combination of waist and panties is made of fine batiste with valenciennes lace and beading. Pink Trousseau ribbon rosettes.

Dainty socklets made of narrow pink Trousseau ribbon. Tiny blue bud in center of knotted rosette. Pink, wide Satin de Luxe makes crown of bonnet. Scalloped turned up brim is made of narrow pink gros grain ribbon, narrow silk lace shirred together and combined with white straw. Small Lady Fair blossoms in all shades of Lady Fair decorate brim. Pink gros grain ribbon used for tie strings.

The Schoolgirl. This party dress is made of peach color taffeta, bound with narrow Silverlast ribbon. Blossom decorations made of Lady Fair ribbon of a peach and rose combination. Hairband made of Silverlast ribbon.

Sport hat and scarf—Brim of hat is made of narrow Tutone satin ribbon faggotted together. Crown of hat is made of wide navy blue Satin de Luxe ribbon. Tassels are formed from narrow Satin de Luxe. Center of scarf is made of wide Tutone satin ribbon, and narrow Tutone ribbons faggotted together on both sides.

The Debutante. Bodice and underdrop made of wide pale pink satin ribbon, overdraped with silver embroidered silk net, bands and edgings of Silverlast ribbon. Decorations of wheels and hanging ends, made of turquoise satin ribbon. Hair band made of turquoise satin ribbon, braided and studded with rhinestones. Flower on side made of rose shadings of satin ribbon.

Novelty pin cushion made of Lady Fair in mais and pink. Dress made of silk lace with narrow Lady Fair ribbon and blossom trim.

Violets for Milady, made of satin ribbon in pretty shades of lavender knotted and stemmed to get desired effect. Green satin leaves give same the finishing touches.

Candy box made of narrow satin ribbon in contrasting shades of rose and pink. Mannequin with lace ruffle adorns corner of box.

Vanity bag made of soft Faille ribbon trimmed with metal lace beading, narrow satin ribbon drawn through beading.

The Hope Chest. One of the happiest stages of a girl's life is the trousseau which this chest contains. Boudoir cap made of pale pink Satin de Luxe combined with narrow silk lace.

Camisole made of pale pink georgette crepe with a top band of pale pink Trousseau ribbon edged with narrow silk lace. Shoulder straps and draw string of 1-inch Lady Fair pink and blue ribbon.

Night gown made of pink crepe de chine tucked with a lace yoke. Lady Fair knotted forms rosettes.

Garters made of pale pink Satin de Luxe ribbon with bowknot of pink and blue Lady Fair.

Slumber slipper case made of Satin de Luxe ribbon in pale blue.

Slippers made of Trousseau ribbon.

Envelope chemise made of pale pink georgette crepe. Narrow pale pink Trousseau ribbon laced through beading. Wide pale pink Trousseau ribbon used for shoulder straps, yoke and on body.

Camisole foundation of pink georgette with mais and pink Lady Fair bowknots. Narrow pink and mais Lady Fair used for shoulder straps and draw string.

Vanity bag made of violet pattern satin ribbon.

The Garters are made of mais Satin de Luxe ribbon, self fringed. Loops and bows of narrow Satin de Luxe.

The Bride. Gown is made of soft white satin, trimmed with looped narrow Satin de Luxe ribbon. Over-train composed of wide Satin de Luxe ribbon, knotted halfway down, being started from the shoulder. Corsage made of Satin de Luxe ribbon blossoms with tiny buds of Silverlast ribbon. Ends for shower bouquet made of knotted Satin de Luxe ribbon. Coronet ornament holding consisting of small orange blossoms, and Silverlast buds, with narrow Satin de Luxe ribbon entwined.

Bridal garters made of narrow Trousseau ribbon, edged with wide silk lace, narrow Trousseau ribbon knotted with centers of Silverlast ribbon to form rosette decoration.

Heart handkerchief case, foundation of white Satin de Luxe ribbon with narrow white Trousseau and silk lace, shirred. Center decoration of knotted Trousseau and Silverlast buds.

The Mother. Negligee made of Dent de Lion color crepe de chine, draped with wide silk lace of same color. Bound and trimmed with meteor blue side pleated Satin de Luxe ribbon. Bows of narrow black velvet ribbon on sides. Cap made of same shade crepe de chine, with lace on sides of same shade, trimmed with narrow meteor Satin de Luxe ribbon and black Alexida velvet ribbon. Rosebud decoration across front.

Baby basket covered with pink Satin de Luxe ribbon, edged with narrow silk lace; decorations of narrow Trousseau ribbon and pink and blue rosebuds. Bow on top of wide Satin de Luxe ribbon. Baby booties made of pale pink Satin de Luxe ribbon, trimmed with narrow lace and narrow ribbon bows.

Baby bunny doll, made of pale grey Satin de Luxe ribbon, stitched in pink. Bow of pink Satin de Luxe ribbon.

The Matron. Entire hat covered with black wide Hyglo ribbon. Loops of narrow black Satin de Luxe ribbon form the only trimming.

Vestee made of wide fancy tinsel ribbon bordering on Gendarme blue. Edge is bound with narrow Gendarme blue Satin de Luxe ribbon. Cut steel buttons are used on same.

Hand bag is made of wide Camisash ribbon in black, stitching and shell frame are of Gendarme blue.

Strap handle bag made of wide black Satin de Luxe ribbon, lined with lavender. Grape effect trimming in center made of Satin de Luxe ribbon in contrasting shades of lavender.

Hand bag, foundation made of wide henna Satin de Luxe ribbon, with narrow black picot edge gros grain ribbon over same. Novelty green gold metal frame used.

Hand bag made of wide fancy ribbon with parachute shape, shell frame. Handle made of narrow Satin de Luxe ribbon.

Vestee made of Persian Jacquard ribbon, with Peter Pan collar of plain Satin de Luxe ribbon to match.

Vestee made of Paisley pattern ribbon, tailormade effect, and black jet buttons.

Ribbon Hats and Beribboned Bags. Entire hat made of two-inch gros grain ribbon of a coral shade shirred on cable cord. Narrow gros grain ribbon used for loops on side. (Lower left.)

Crown of hat made of one-inch delft blue gros grain ribbon lattice worked. Brim made of a Persian pattern ribbon bordering on the delft blue shade. Narrow blue gros grain ribbon, box pleated, adorns front of brim. (Lower right.)

Crown and brim of hat covered with wide Hyglo ribbon in a pretty henna shade. Narrow Satin Tutone ribbon in black and henna crocheted about brim and across crown. ((Upper.)

Taupe grey evening bag, made of Satin de Luxe ribbon, basket effect; grape trimming made of Satin de Luxe ribbon in contrasting shades of blue. Hand strings made of narrow Satin de Luxe ribbon.

Hand bag built from Persian wide fancy ribbon with plain navy blue Democracy gros grain ribbon; metal frame used.

FROM OUR NOVELTY SHOP

1. Three-cornered pillow made of wide Persian pattern ribbon, combined with narrow shirred Satin de Luxe and narrow fancy ribbon.
2. Sweet grass sewing basket lined with old rose Satin de Luxe ribbon. Apple decoration made of satin ribbon.
3. Lamp shade, made of Satin de Luxe ribbon in old rose, narrow satin ribbon in a darker shade used for shirring. Floral trimming made in colors on rose and lavender in Satin de Luxe.
4. Trinket box—Satin de Luxe in different widths, in pretty rose colorings, shirred about box. Bud trimming of contrasting shades of lavender.
5. Work basket—Basket covered with Capri Camisash ribbon. Lining of contrasting shade. Variegated flower trimming.

6. Vanity bag made of pretty shades of red Satin de Luxe. Flower trimming and buds decorate the entire article.
7. Novelty work bag made of wide Sankanac ribbon, in old rose, bound with narrow black satin ribbon.
8. Para pillow made of tucked black satin ribbon, two inches wide, combined with fancy brocade ribbon.
9. Boudoir light Skirt made of wide Satin de Luxe ribbon in jackrose, overskirt and bodice made of Satin de Luxe in contrasting color. Trimmings of silk lace and variegated flowers.
10. Telephone cover and light in one, made of Satin de Luxe ribbon, rose colorings. Overskirt made of Hyglo ribbon in rose. Narrow satin ribbon bow decorations in pale lavender.

Fifth Avenue This Season
is Literally
A Ribbon Parade

TAKE A STROLL UP FIFTH AVENUE ANY OF THESE
FINE DAYS, AND WATCH WHAT MIGHT BE APTLY
TERMED, THE RIBBON PARADE! THE FROCKS AND
HATS ON THESE PAGES NOW OPENING BEFORE
YOU ARE FAIR EXAMPLES OF WHAT ONE MAY
PASS EITHER ON THE SHAPELY FIGURE OF SOME
PROMINENT MEMBER OF NEW YORK'S SOCIAL
WORLD OR IN THE SMART MODISTE SHOPS ON
FIFTH AVENUE, WHICH ARE TRULY MAKING PARIS
LOOK TO HER LAURELS IF SHE WOULD MAINTAIN
HER PRESTIGE AS QUEEN OF FASHIONS. BOTH
PARIS AND NEW YORK HAVE DECREED RIBBONS ON
STREET, AFTERNOON AND EVENING CREATIONS,
AND IF YOU WOULD BE CHIC, JUST REMEMBER TO
OBEY THE MANDATE.

Face to face with
Ribbons
on the Boulevards
of Paris

FACE TO FACE WITH RIBBONS! THAT DESCRIBES
THIS SEASON ON THE FASHIONABLE BOULEVARDS
OF PARIS. ONCE AGAIN THE LOOMS OF THE RIB-
BON MAKERS ARE AT WORK, THEIR WONDERS TO
PERFORM, AND, PRESTO! BEHOLD THE PARISIAN
CREATIONS ON THESE TWO PAGES. RIBBONS, RIB-
BONS, EVERYWHERE! CATCH THE PARISIAN TOUCH
RIBBON GIVES TO THESE GOWNS, AND THEIR
SMARTNESS IS YOURS IF YOU HAVE THE ENERGY
TO STUDY THEIR LINES AND TO VISIT THE RIBBON
COUNTER.

The Spirit of Ribbon

I am Ribbon.

I am the flowing sheen of the Orient, cultured and woven in the Occident, and worn wherever women desire to make themselves beautiful.

Ornament itself, am I.

With my aid, the humblest of Femininity may be regaled in the garnitures of an Eastern Queen.

With the precision of a surgeon do I probe the Soul of Beauty through the Eye, portraying each Devotee to the High Priestess as an Archangel of Mystic Beauty.

I am Ribbon.

I am Colors.   Greens, reds, yellows, blues and blacks, mingle within my Texture, fading themselves into pinks and pearls, and grays, glorifying the humblest textures of my woven sisters.

In Me are all the arts glorified, the colors of Literature, Painting, Sculpture, Music and Dancing.   I show the spirit of comedy, the glamour of romance; even the veiled figure of tragedy.   I am Fantasy and Realism combined.

I am Ribbon.

I first came Occidentalwards in the Dark days of Feudalism and became the first of the Lighter Graces to cheer the Dawn of Modernity. The Flower of Knighthood began to bloom in designs and the looms of the Fleur de Lis of France saw me rise to a height of splendor from which I cannot fall.

In stately procession my devotees, the Ages of Dress, pass by, and so Today arrives.

Look ye then, at any passing child, girl or woman and somewhere, adding lustre to nature, you will see Me.·

I am Ribbon.